LEWISHAM TO DARTFORD
via Bexleyheath and Sidcup

Vic Mitchell and Keith Smith

Vic Mitchell

MP Middleton Press

Cover picture: On 23rd May 1959, class D1 4-4-0 no.31743 was recorded at Dartford, bearing the "Via Dartford Loop" headcode. A North Kent or Bexleyheath Line electric service has terminated on the right. (A.E.Bennett)

First published September 1991

ISBN 0 906520 92 4

© *Middleton Press 1991*

Design - Deborah Goodridge
Laser typesetting - Barbara Mitchell

Published by Middleton Press
          Easebourne Lane
          Midhurst
          West Sussex
          Tel: (0730) 813169

Printed & bound by Biddles Ltd,
          Guildford and Kings Lynn

CONTENTS

92	Albany Park
49	Barnehurst
96	Bexley
44	Bexleyheath
7	Blackheath
106	Crayford
114	Dartford
28	Eltham
30	Eltham Park
21	Eltham Well Hall
36	Falconwood
56	Hither Green
16	Kidbrooke
65	Lee
1	Lewisham
73	Mottingham
77	New Eltham
85	Sidcup
54	Slade Green
39	Welling

ACKNOWLEDGEMENTS

We are immensely grateful for assistance and information received from the photographers mentioned in the captions and also from R.M.Casserley, C.R.L.Coles, I.Gotheridge, N.Langridge, A.Ll.Lambert, Network South East Public Relations, R.Randell, G.T.V.Stacey, E.Staff, N.Stanyon, D.Monk-Steel and our ever supportive wives.

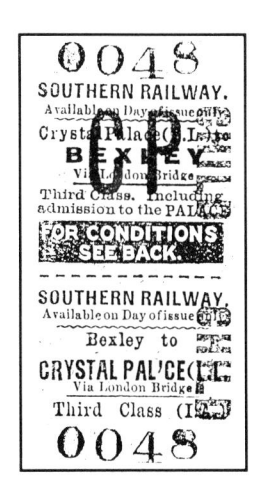

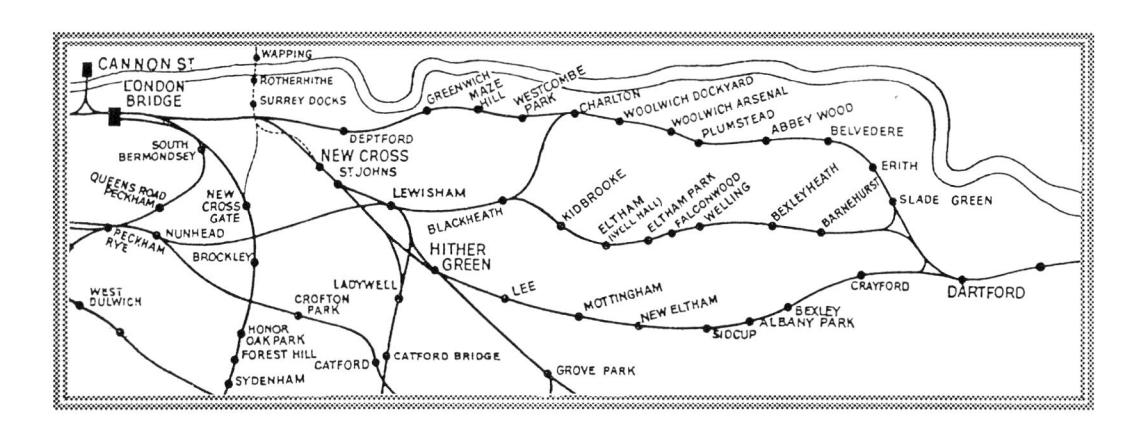

GEOGRAPHICAL SETTING

Lewisham is situated in the valley of the Bourne which enters the River Thames at Deptford Creek. Both routes climb to traverse London Clay and Blackheath Beds, which are composed of sand and pebbles. The Sidcup line reaches the Cray Valley at Bexley and the Bexleyheath trains cross the River Cray one mile west of Dartford. After the routes converge, the line passes through a chalk cutting before descending into the Darent Valley at Dartford, the station being situated close to a bridge over the river.

All maps are to the scale of 25" to 1 mile, unless otherwise stated.

This 1914 map at 1" to 1 mile includes a roads revision to 1929 and hence part of the Rochester Way completed in 1923-24 to relieve congestion in Bexleyheath (officially spelt as one word since 1894). On the left, the word "Lewisham" is close to Lady Well station, Lewisham station being ¾ mile to the north. A close study reveals that few housing estates had appeared east of Lee and Blackheath, prior to World War I. These proliferated in the 1930s.

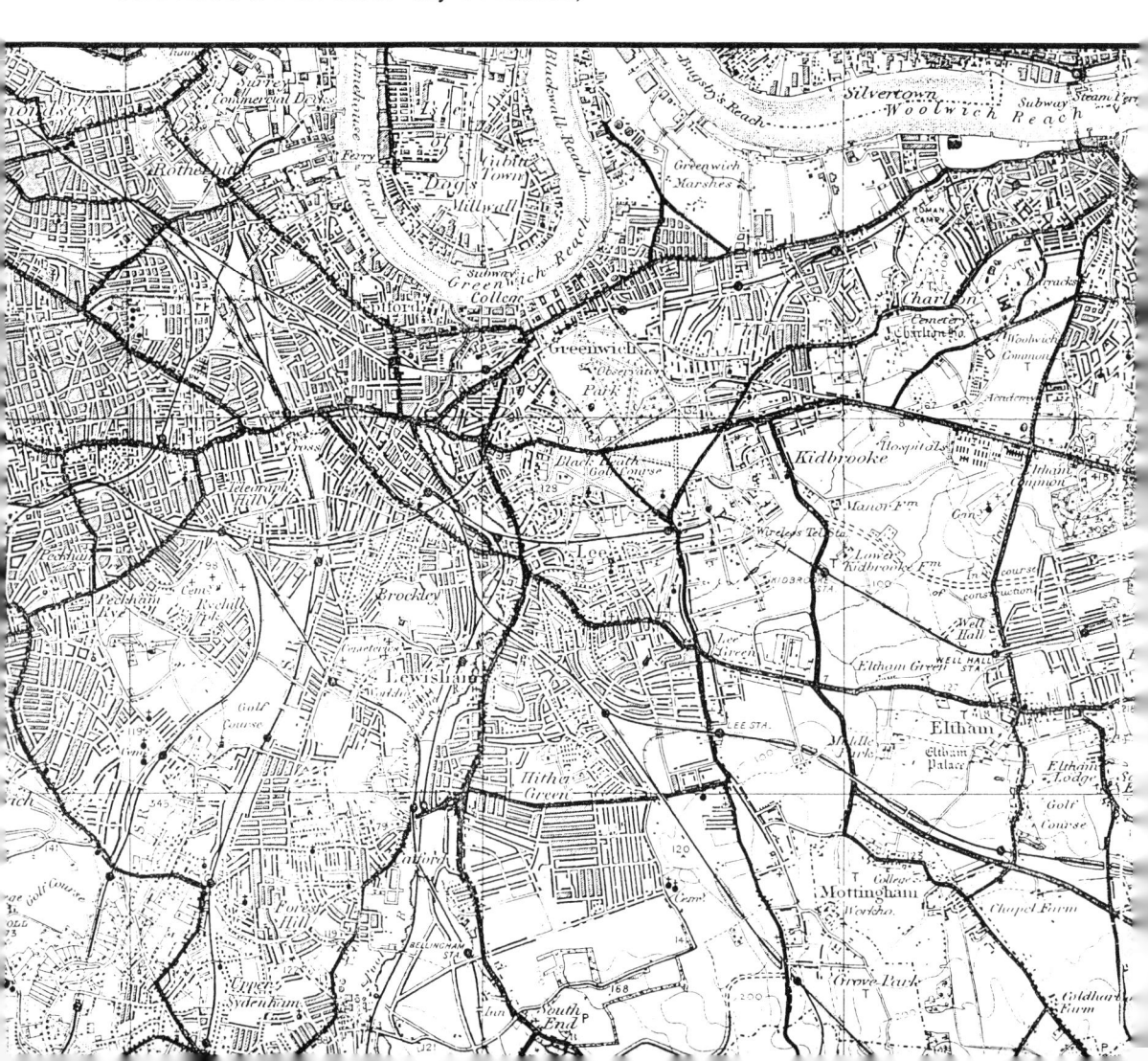

HISTORICAL BACKGROUND

The first railway between London and Dartford was the North Kent line, which ran via Lewisham, Blackheath and Woolwich. It opened on 30th July 1849, trains terminating at Rochester (now Strood station). The deviation south through Blackheath was necessary as the Astronomer Royal refused to allow trains near the Greenwich Observatory at that time.

To reduce congestion on the North Kent Line and to give a more direct route between London and Dartford (also to open up new country), a line via Sidcup was opened on 1st September 1866. This branched from the 1865 railway between Lewisham and Chislehurst at Hither Green, although there was no station there until 1895. The route became known as the "Dartford Loop" and has recently been redesignated less confusingly as the "Sidcup Line", the term thus being used throughout this book.

The network described was operated by the South Eastern Railway who were approached by a group of landowners who felt that they would benefit financially from the presence of a railway parallel to the Sidcup Line and the North Kent. A cool response resulted in the formation of an independent company and the passing of the Bexley Heath Railway Act on 20th August 1883. After protracted arguments lasting many years, the SER agreed to be involved in financing the line and to operate it. Following problems with unstable clay cuttings and embankments, the Bexleyheath →

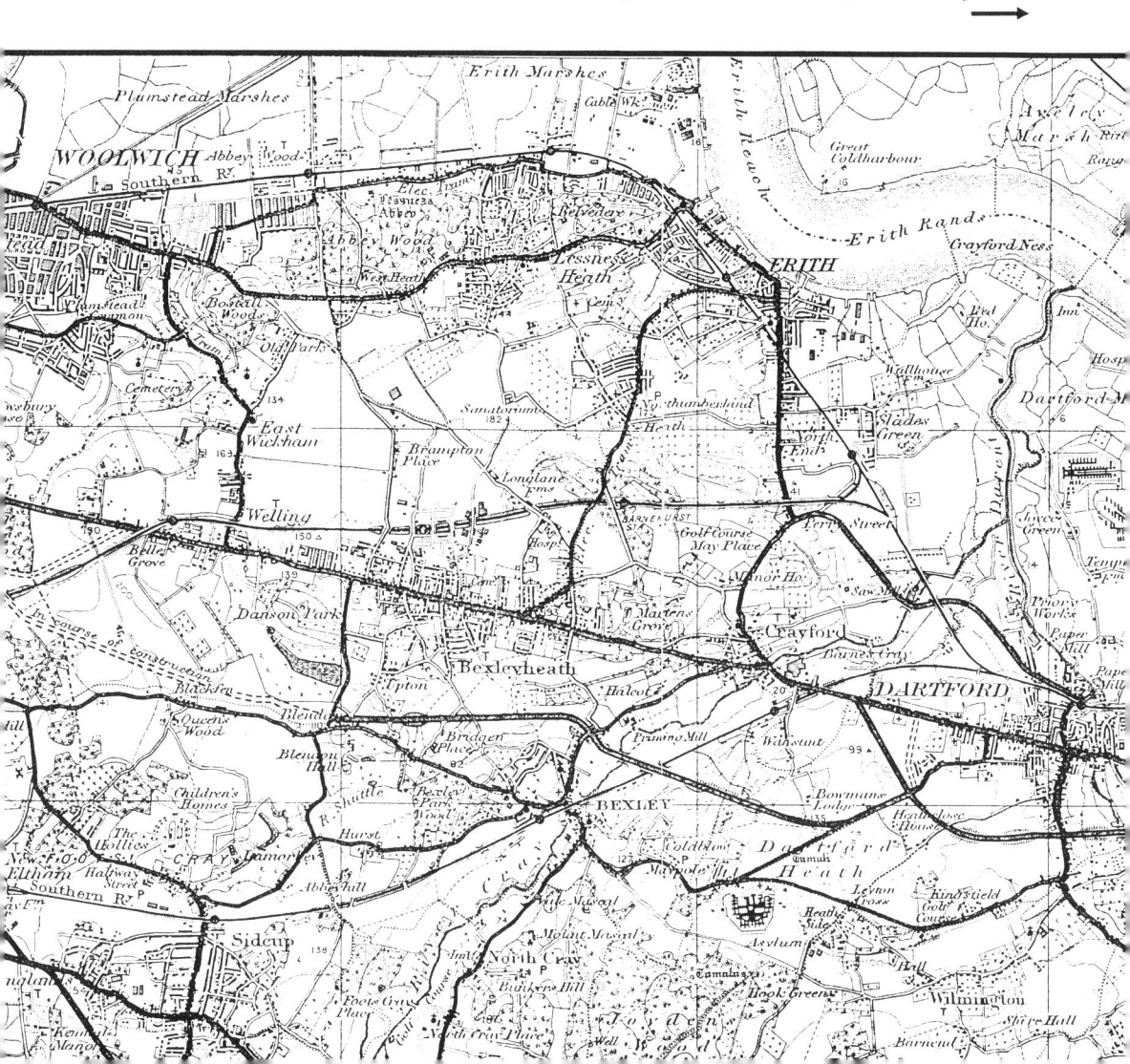

Line came into use on 1st May 1895. The anticipated increase in land values followed, as housing development took place around the then country stations.

From 1899, the routes were operated by the South Eastern & Chatham Railway; from 1923 by the Southern Railway and since 1948 by British Railways. The most significant event this century was the introduction of electric traction to both routes on 6th June 1926, although the full electric service did not start until 12th July of that year. (Some electric trains were reported to have run during the General Strike - 10th to 16th May).

PASSENGER SERVICES

The figures quoted refer to down trains, the up timetable being generally similar.

Bexleyheath Line

Upon opening, there were nine trains, weekdays only, this increasing to nineteen within four years. Of these, five terminated at Dartford, six at Erith, and the remainder intermediately.

By 1913 weekday frequency had increased to 24, with half running to Dartford. Twelve ran on Sundays, all but one to Dartford. By the end of steam traction, there were over 30 weekday journeys, but many were running to Erith instead of Dartford.

Sidcup Line

Initially there were eleven weekday trains, this increasing to twelve by 1869, when there were also five on Sundays. By 1890, the figures were 19 and 5 respectively. The 1906 timetable showed 26 weekday trains covering the full length of the route, most stopping at all stations. One peak hour train terminated at Crayford and there were 14 Sunday journeys.

In 1916, 31 through trains were shown, several business journeys skipping some intermediate stops. There were 14 Sunday trains, the 8.54pm from Hither Green running non-stop to Dartford.

The last steam operated timetable contained 37 stopping trains, two of which terminated at Crayford. Sunday traffic was still handled by 14 trains.

Electrification

Electrification in 1926 brought a basic 30 minute interval service on both routes (hourly on Sundays) but through running beyond Dartford ceased. In the steam era, regular destinations had included Maidstone and New Brompton (now Gillingham). To compensate for this, journey times were reduced by about one third and over 70 trains were provided on each route on weekdays. Extension of electrification to Gravesend in 1930 restored some through running eastward.

In order to reduce congestion on peak hour Cannon Street services, some extra trains were operated to and from Holborn Viaduct and/or Blackfriars from 30th July 1935 until World War II, and again from 12th August 1946.

The table below indicates the basic service interval in minutes for representative years.

	Bexleyheath Line		Sidcup Line	
	Weekdays	Sundays	Weekdays	Sundays
1931	15	15	30	30
1938	15	15	15	15
1944	30	60	30	60
1949	15	15	15	15
1958	15	30	15	30
1969	15	30	15	30
1980	20	30	20	30

On 1st June 1981, a daily half-hourly timetable was introduced. Since 1986, there has been a peak hour service between Barnehurst and Victoria. The one Sidcup Line train to Victoria, also introduced in 1986, was withdrawn in May 1988.

STATIONS.	1 & 2 Class. P M	1 2 3 Class. P M	1 2 3 Class. P M	1 2 3 Class. P M	1 2 3 Class. P M	1 2 3 Class. P M	1 2 3 Class. P M	1 2 3 Class. P M	1 2 3 Class. P M	1 2 3 Class P M	1 2 3 Class. P M	1 2 3 Class. P M
Charing Cross. ....dep.	4 42	..	4 55	..	5 17	..	5 33	..	5 45	5 48	..	..
Waterloo Junction „	4 44	..	4 57	..	5 19	..	..	..	5 47	..	..	..
Cannon Street......... „	4 52	4 55	5 6	5 15	5 27	5 35	5 40	5 45	5 54	..	6 0	6 15
London Bridge ...... „	4 56	4 58	5 10	5 19	..	5 39	5 44	..	5 57	5 55	6 4	6 20
Spa Road.............. „	..	..	..	..	..	..	..	..	..	..	..	..
Bricklayers' Arms...dep.	..	..	..	..	..	..	..	..	..	..	..	..
New Cross............arr.	..	5 7	..	5 27	..	5 46	..	..	..	6 2	6 12	6 27
Park's Bridge Junc. pass	5 6	..	5 20	..	..	5 48	..	..	6 7	..	..	6 30
Hither Green Junc.... „	5 7	..	..	..	..	5 49	..	..		..	..	6 32
Lee ....arr.	5 10	..		..	..	5 52	..	..		..	..	6 35
Eltham .... „	5 14	..	Loop Line.	..	..	5 56	..	..	Via Lady Well Loop.	..	..	6 40
Sidcup .... „	5 20	..		..	..	6 2	..	..		..	..	6 46
Bexley .... „	5 25	..		..	..	6 8	..	..		..	..	6 52
Crayford .... „	5 30	..		..	..	6 14	..	..		..	..	6 58
Lewisham Junction ...arr.	..	5 11	..	5 31	5 40	..	..	5 57	..	6 6	6 16	..
Lady Well ....arr.	..	..	5 21	..	..	..	..	..	6 6	..	..	..
Catford Bridge......... „	..	..	5 25	..	..	..	..	..	6 9	..	..	..
Lower Sydenham ...... „	..	..	..	..	..	..	..	..	6 12	..	..	..
New Beckenham ...... „	..	..	5 32	..	..	..	..	..	6 15	..	..	..
New Beckenham ......dep.	..	..	5 33	..	..	..	..	..	6 16	..	..	..
Elmer's End ....arr.	..	..	5 36	..	..	..	..	..	6 21	..	..	..
Croydon (Add. R.) ... „	..	..	5 41	..	..	..	..	..	6 25	..	..	..
Beckenham Junction....arr.	..	..	5 40	..	..	..	..	..	6 26	..	..	..
Blackheath ....arr.		5 15	..	5 35	5 43		..	6 0	..	6 10	6 19	
Charlton ....arr.		5 22	..	..	5 49		..	..	..	..	6 26	
Woolwich Dockyard .. „		5 26	..	..	5 53		6 4	..	..	..	6 30	
Woolwich Arsenal { arr.	Via Dartford Loop.	5 30	..	..	5 56	Via Dartford Loop.	6 8	..	..	..	6 34	Via Dartford Loop.
{ dep.		..	..	..	..		6 9	..	..	..	6 36	
Plumstead...............arr.		..	..	..	..		..	..	..	..	6 39	
Abbey Wood .... „		..	..	..	..		6 14	..	..	..	6 44	
Belvedere .... „		..	..	..	..		6 18	..	..	..	6 49	
Erith................ „		..	..	..	..		6 21	..	..	..	6 52	
Dartford { arr.	5 35	..	..	..	..	6 20	6 29	..	..	..	7 1	7 5
{ dep.	5 37	..	..	..	..		6 31	..	..	..	..	7 7
Greenhithe ....arr.	5 43	..	..	..	..		6 37	..	..	..	..	7 14
Northfleet.............. „	5 48	..	..	..	..		6 42	..	..	..	..	7 20
Gravesend { arr.	5 53	..	..	..	..		6 47	..	..	..	..	7 25
{ dep	5 55	..	..	..	..		6 49	..	..	..	..	
Higham ....arr.	..	..	..	..	..		6 59	..	..	..	..	..
Strood { arr.	6 8	..	..	..	..		7 7	..	..	..	..	..
{ dep.	6 10	..	..	..	..		..	..	..	..	..	..
Cuxton ....arr.	6 17	..	..	..	..		..	..	..	..	..	..
Snodland .... „	6 23	..	..	..	..		..	..	..	..	..	..
Aylesford .... „	6 29	..	..	..	..		..	..	..	..	..	..
Maidstone .... „	6 40	..	..	..	..		..	..	..	..	..	..

May 1870 peak hour down weekday timetable.

FREIGHT SERVICES

The working timetable for June 1956 has been selected as representative of local traffic arrangements before the decline of the 1960s.

```
Notes:-
   EWD  :  Every Week Day
   F    :  Freight Train
   L/E  :  Light Engine (also shown by // between timings)
   /    :  between timings indicates passing time.
```

Load Days Run		F MO am	F MO am	F EWD am	SF MX am	L/E MO am	F EWD am	MILK MX am	F EWD am	L/E MX am	L/E MO am	F SX am	F SO am	F SX am	F SX Q am	L/E SO am
Bricklayers Arms	dep			12.40	2.10											11//
Clapham Junction	dep							2.35								
HITHER GREEN	dep		12.40			3//30	3.55					9.16	9.16	10.6	10.43	
Lee	arr		12/50		2/30		4/5					9.28 10.5	9.28 9.52	10/16	10/49	
Mottingham	arr dep	PM 11.30		1.10 1.40	2/35	*//*			3.14	4.23		10.12	9.58	10/21	10/55	11//
New Eltham	arr dep		12/56				4/15									
Sidcup	arr dep			1/48						4.33 4.48			Runs from 22.9.56				
Bexley	arr dep															
Crayford	arr dep	11.50 12.15 am			2/49		4/31			4.58				10/36	11/11	
Vickers Siding	arr dep										5//18	5//40				
Crayford Spur B														10/39	11/14	
Northend Sidings	arr											Via Slade Green			11.35	
Erith	arr															
PLUMSTEAD	arr													11.26		
Eltham Well Hall	arr															
Blackheath	arr															
DARTFORD	arr		12.20	1.20	2.7	2/56 3.22	4/39 5.8			5//23	6//0					
HOO JUNCTION	arr															

Load Days Run			F MX PM	F MX PM	F EWD PM	F MX PM	L/E EWD am	F EWD am	F EWD am	L/E SX am	L/B SO am	L/E SX am	L/E am	F SX am	MILK SO PM	F SX am	L/E EWD PM
Dover	dep 1					8.0											
Maidstone West	dep 2				11.40												
Queenborough	dep 3																
HOO JUNCTION	dep 4		11.30		am	am		3.10	4.22				10//30	10.46		11.40	12//
DARTFORD	dep 5		12/0		1/15	1/55		4/15	4.48			9//48	10//44		11/12		12/12
Angersteins Wharf	dep 6																
PLUMSTEAD	dep 7							6//0									
Erith	dep 8				11.38												
Northend Sidings	dep 9				am												
Crayford Spur B	10				12/10												
Crayford	arr 11 dep		12/5	12/15	am	2/0		4/20						11.17			
Bexley	arr 12 dep																
Sidcup	arr 13 dep		12/19	12/29				4/35	5/6								
New Eltham	arr 14 dep																
Mottingham	arr 15 dep		12/25		1/40	2/20	3//30	4/41							12.03		
Lee Junction	arr 16 dep				12/40	1/45	2/24		4/45	5/20						PM 12/39		
HITHER GREEN	arr 17				12.50	1.55	2.35	3//45	4.55	5.30	6//48	10//25	11//13	11//30		12.45	12/
Bricklayers Arms	arr 18																
Herne Hill	arr 19	1.17															
Clapham Junction	arr 20														12.45		
Willesden	arr 21																

Load Days Run		F MX	LE EWD	LE MX	LE MX	F SO	F SX	F SX	F SX
		PM	am	am	am	PM	PM	PM	PM
Dartford	dep			5//27					
Crayford	dep	11.54					4//53	9//20	
		am							
North End Sidings	dep				5//30 Via C!f'd Creek				
Braby's Siding	arr	12.9							
	dep	12.55							
Barnehurst	arr			5//33	5//55				
Bexleyheath	arr	1/9						9//29	
	dep					4.42			
Eltham Well Hall	arr	1/20				4.53	5//15		
	dep		2//45			6.25	8.8		
Kidbrooke	arr								10.7
	dep								
Blackheath	arr	1.35	3//0			6.33	8.18		10.15

Load Days Run		F EWD	F EWD	LE MX	LE MX	F SO	F SX	F SX	EBV SX
		am	am	am	am	PM	PM	PM	PM
Blackheath	dep	2.0	3.32			3.25	7.26		9.25
Kidbrooke	arr		3.37						9.30
	dep		3.50						
Eltham Well Hall	arr	2.12				3/35	7/37		
	dep								
Welling	arr		3.56						
	dep		4.50						
Bexleyheath	arr					3.50	7.51		
	dep						9//15	9.40	
Barnehurst	arr		5.0	5//34	5//55				
	dep		5.20						
Dartford	arr						10//0		
North End Sidings	arr		5/32	5//52				9.53	
Erith	arr				6//3				
Plumstead	arr		5.50						

F SX PM	F SX PM	F SO PM	F SO PM	L/E EWD PM	F SX PM	F SO PM	F SO PM	F SX PM	F SX PM	F SX PM	F SO PM	F SX PM	F SO PM	F SO PM	F SX PM	F SX PM	F SO Q PM	F SX
.20	2.10	2.20	2.40	4//0	4.16		6.24	7.5	7.5	7.23	7.24	8.10	9.10	9.55		11.35		
/33	2/18	2/33	2/48		4/25		6/33	7/15	7/15	7/33	7/34	8/19	9/20	10/5		11/45		
/39	2.26	2/39	2.56		4.33		6/40	7/21	7.23	7/39	7/40	8/25			10.24	11/51	11.42	
	3.5					6.10												
		2/46				6.17	6/48	7/28		7/46				10/31		11/49		
						7.14												
/55	3.21	2/55		4//22		7.22	6/56	7/37		7/55	7/56	8/39	9/38	10/27	10.41	12.10	11/54	
	12.19			4//53											11.25	1.10		11.54
															11.28			11.57
															11.43			11.59
/58		2/58					6/59	7/40		7/58	7/59			10/30		1/18	11/58	
.27		3.28					7.28		8.13		8.13	9.13			11.14		1.45	
				5//15	Until 14.9.56		From 22.9.56	To 14.9.56	From 17.9.56	From 17.9.56							1.30	1.35
	12/29											8/47	9/46		11.51			
	1.20											9.15	10.14					

ILK X M	F SX PM	F SX PM	F SX PM	F SX PM	F SO PM	F SO PM	F SO PM	F SX PM	F SO PM	F SO PM	F SO PM	F SO PM	F MSX PM	F MO PM	L/E PM	F SO PM	F SO PM	F SO PM	F SO PM
											7.5					7.24		10.30		9.10 am
				3.5		4.40	6.42	7.11				8.11	10/8	10.25	10.25	10//52	10/58	10/58		12/5
				3/32		5/11	7/11							10/53	10/53					Sun
		1.30							7.10		7.30					Via Crayford Creek			10.40	
	1.30							6.42 Hoo												
		1/48	3/0						8/2		8/2						From 22.9.56	11.14		Until 16.9.56
			3/3	3/37				when Q Runs.						10.59	11//6			11.22		
					4.36				8.17					11.1						
					4.42			run	8.23											
					5.15			not	9.6											
				3/16	3/49	5.20		will					11/12	11/16		11/17	11/17			
						7.40														
						7.45		to Willesden												
						8.43			9.18											
									10.10											
2.50	2/9	3/22	3/57	8.50				7/36		8/36		11/18	11/24		11/23	11/23	11/46	12/30		
					9.19															
			3/26	4/1	9/24	5/40	7/39	7/40	8/25	10/17	8/25	8/40	10/35	11/22	11/29		11/28	11/28	11/51	12/36
	2.20	3.35	4.12	9.34	5.50		7.50	8.35	10.25	8.35	8.50	10.45	11.30	11.38		11.38	11.59			
															11.55				1.10	
.20					9.35															

Bexleyheath Line

LEWISHAM

1. Initially, Lewisham was an intermediate station on the London Bridge to Woolwich line, opening on 30th July 1849. It became a junction station when the line to Beckenham (visible in the background) came into use on 1st January 1857. (Lens of Sutton)

The 1st edition of the Ordnance Survey was published in about 1862 and has the line to Blackheath on the right. Also on the right is Granville Park siding. This was used mainly for coal and was closed on 6th May 1963, having been served by the 4.20am Bricklayers Arms to Angerstein Wharf service in later years.

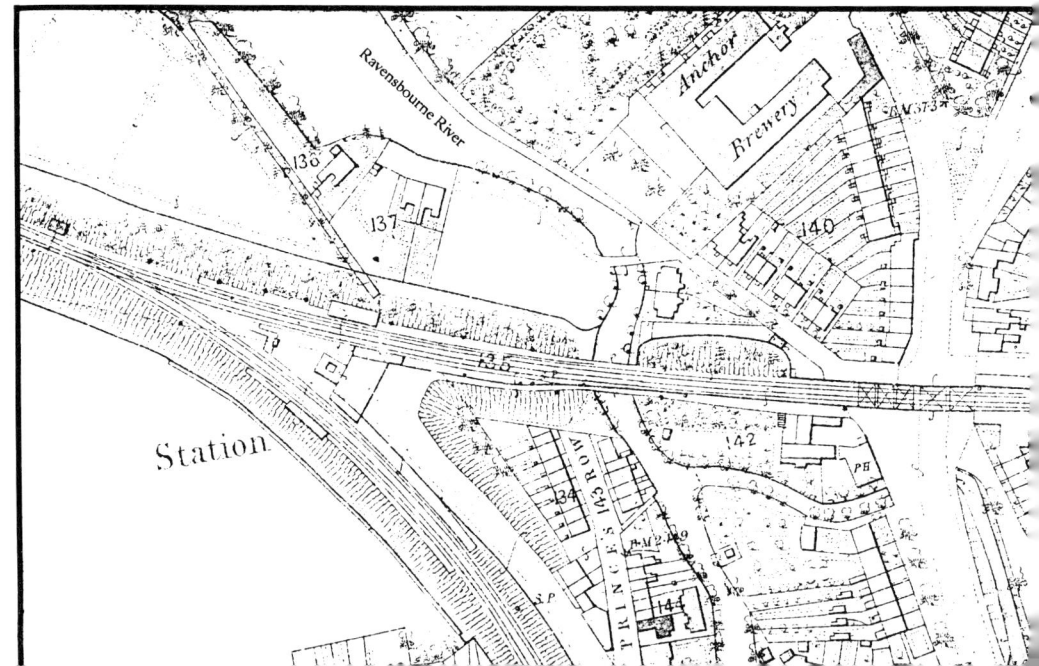

2. This was the vista presented to a passenger alighting from an up Bexleyheath line train in the 1950s. On the right is the original route to London Bridge, trains to Blackfriars and Holborn Viaduct having used the route over the bridge since 1935. This had been brought into use in 1929 for freight services.
(Lens of Sutton)

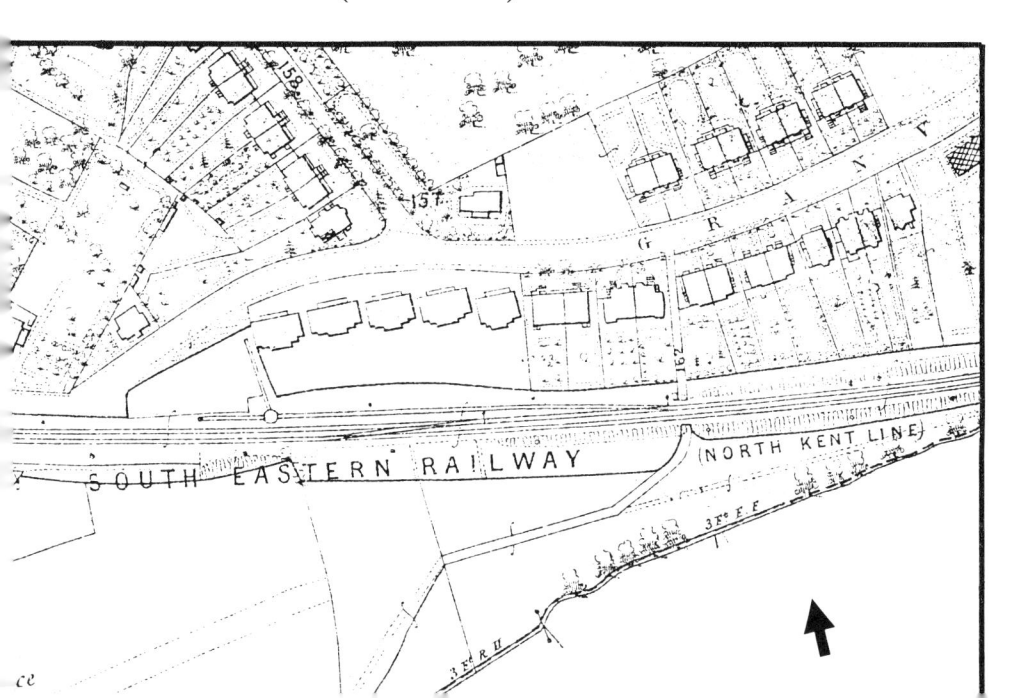

3. The Railway Correspondence and Travel Society "London River" railtour passes Lewisham on the final leg (Blackheath to Liverpool Street via the Thames Tunnel) of its journey on 29th March 1958. It had begun at London Bridge and had included the Bricklayers Arms, Angerstein Wharf and Deptford Wharf lines. Ex-GER Class J68 0-6-0T no.68646 is hauling one ex-LSWR vehicle and two ex-SECR ones. (N.Sprinks)

4. Having passed through platform 3, no.33049 proceeds towards Nunhead with the diverted 09.10 Sheerness Steel Works to Willesden Speedlink service on 23rd October 1986. The POA wagons had conveyed scrap steel used for the production of reinforcing rods and coils. (C.Wilson)

5. On the same day, nos.33203 and 33209 approach platform 4 with empty aggregate wagons from Purley and Salfords, bound for the Brett Marine terminal at Cliffe on the Isle of Grain. See picture no.91 in our *East Croydon to Three Bridges* album and no. 20 in *Branch Line to Allhallows* to complete the journey. (C.Wilson)

> **Other views of this station are included in the companion album** *Holborn Viaduct to Lewisham.*

6. The offices and entrance are under the roof on the left of this 1990 westward view. The old buildings were largely intact, although subject to modernisation in 1983. "Lewisham Junction" was the official name from 1857 until 1929. (J.Scrace)

BLACKHEATH

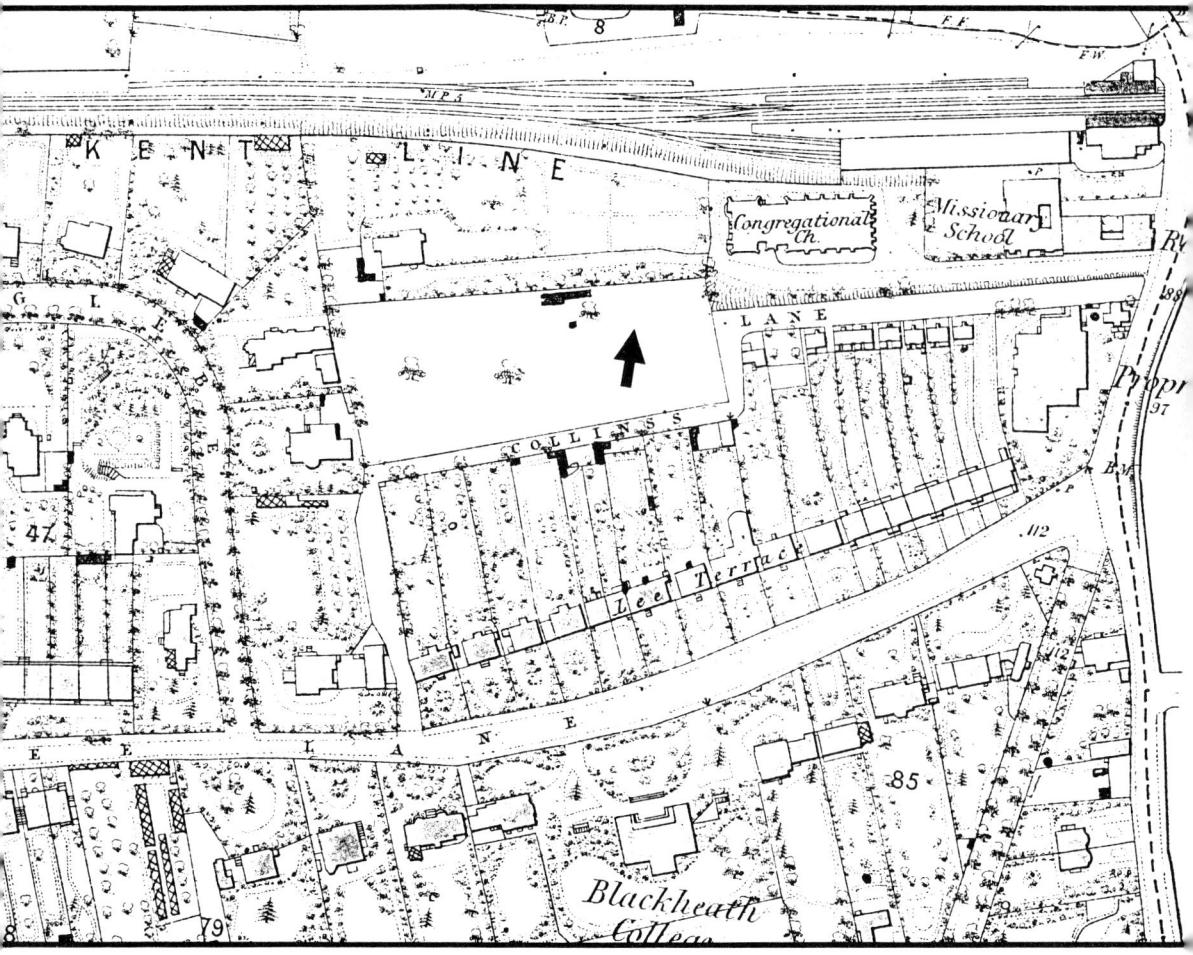

As at Lewisham, the station opened with the circuitous route to Woolwich on 30th July 1849 and high quality housing development followed, as this map from the 1860s shows. Note the avenues of trees and spacious gardens. The bay platform line and two adjacent tracks are roofed over - presumably a carriage shed for local trains.

By the time of this 1916 edition, the goods yard had been expanded, with a goods shed and 9-ton crane. Some of the sidings were used for carriage berthing and others for freight sorting.

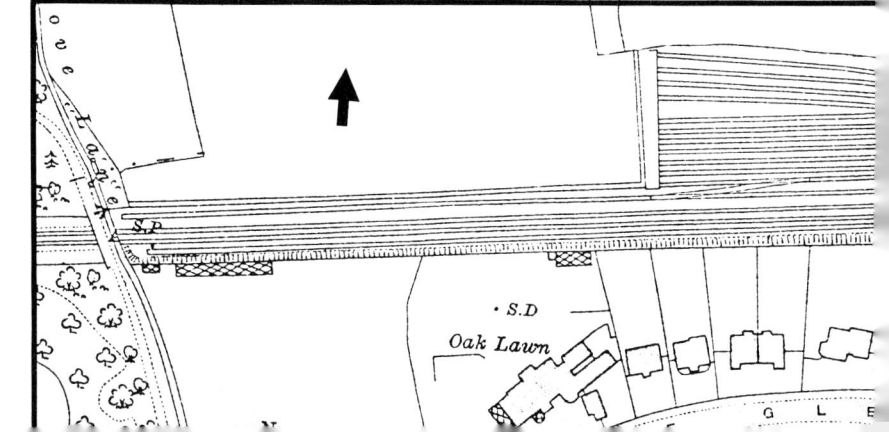

7. The station entrance was (and is) conveniently situated to the shops between Lee Road and Tranquil Vale - an apt name in the pre-railway age. The no.75 bus is bound for Croydon. (Lens of Sutton)

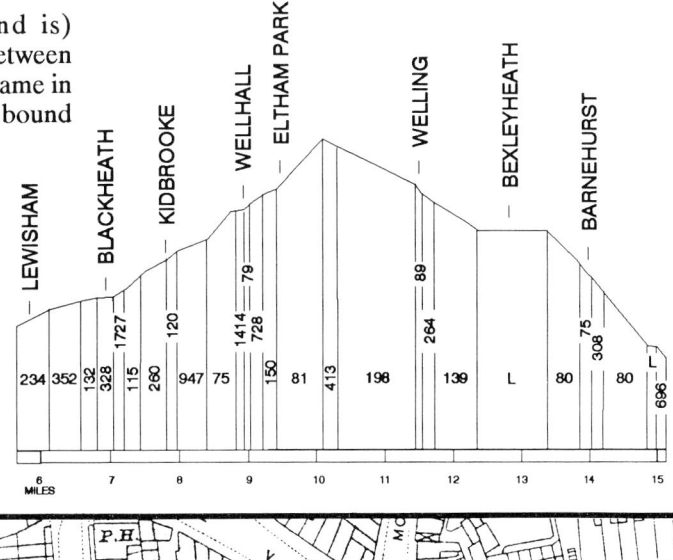

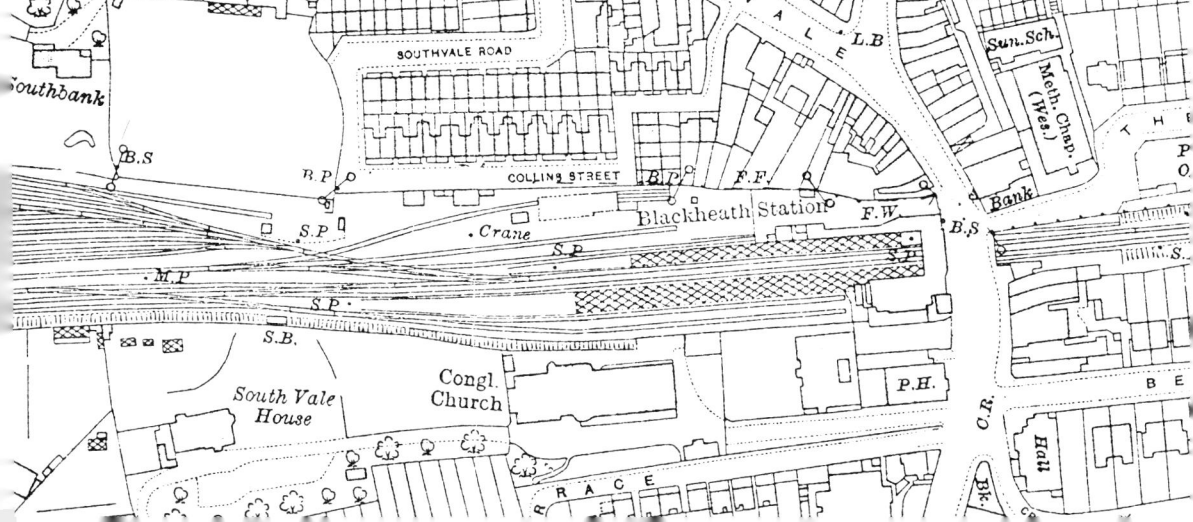

8. An eastward view in 1923 includes details of the elegant gas lamp, with its "barley sugar" post and the shunt signal, which controlled access to the down sidings. Signals were seldom mounted on lampposts. (H.J.Patterson-Rutherford)

9. There were twelve parallel sidings on the down side, the first pair being connected with two crossovers but none were electrified. King Arthur class no. 30800 *Sir Meleaus de Lile* is in no. 2 road on 26th August 1956. The following year DEMUs were stored here, prior to their introduction on the Charing Cross - Hastings service. (A.E.Bennett)

10. The railtour seen in picture no.3 changed locomotives in the bay platform, little used since electrification. The locomotive by the buffers is H class 0-4-4T no. 31518. (S.C.Nash)

11. For many years, the siding by the wall accommodated the weed killing train, the area around the rails being partially paved. The train comprised two former parcel vans, six adapted locomotive tenders and a brake van, visible in the previous photograph. (J.N.Faulkner)

12. The location of this box is shown on the 1916 map but it was designated "B" Box until 1929, when "A" Box (further west) was abolished. Both Blackheath boxes were closed on 15th March 1970. (J.Scrace)

13. "B" Box ("C" until 1929) controlled the junction between the North Kent and Bexleyheath Lines and is seen in July 1969. The retaining wall beyond it continues east of the bridge, as far as the 437yd Kidbrooke Tunnel. Both were necessary to appease local landowners - a continuous wide cutting would have been preferable. (J.Scrace)

14. The 1970 junction signal is seen at the back of the station building. The down canopy was still standing in 1991 but the up one was demolished in 1985. Goods facilities were withdrawn on 6th May 1963. (C.Hall)

15. Prior to being photographed in 1990, the exterior had been cleaned and fitted with new lettering and an old diamond-shaped bridge weight restriction sign, referring to "heavy motor cars" etc. (J.Scrace)

KIDBROOKE

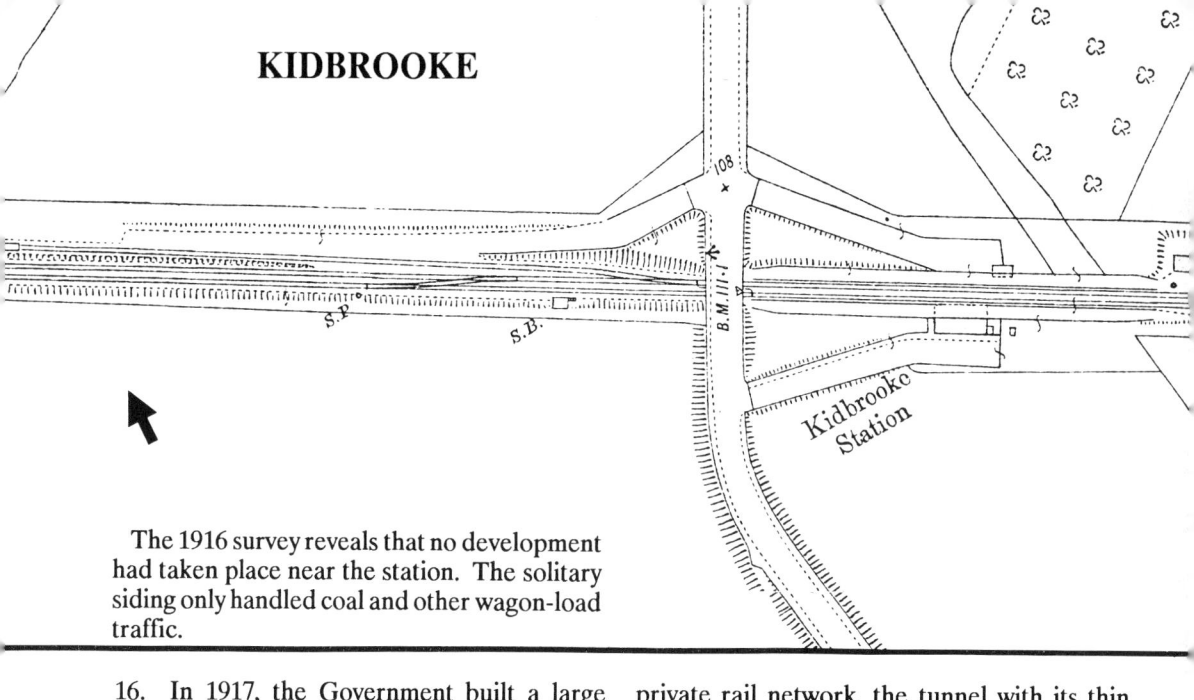

The 1916 survey reveals that no development had taken place near the station. The solitary siding only handled coal and other wagon-load traffic.

16. In 1917, the Government built a large storage depot south of the line, the RAF being the main user. This westward view from the road bridge includes the gates to the depot's private rail network, the tunnel with its thin covering and the single public siding, complete with loading gauge.
(H.J.Patterson-Rutherford)

17. Looking south-east from the bridge, we see more of the extensive depot, along with the sidings on this part of the site. The number of passengers arriving to work at the stores often exceeded the number departing to toil in London. (H.J.Patterson-Rutherford)

18. The signal box was situated opposite the points to the public siding, which remained in use until 7th October 1968. The box closed on 14th March 1970, when colour light signalling was introduced on the route. (J.Scrace)

19. Being one of the least used stations on the line, it was the last to be rebuilt, retaining its original structure and gas lights until 1972 although the footbridge had been replaced in 1954. (J.Scrace)

20. This and the previous picture were taken in 1990 and show railway architecture at its low point, when the CLASP system was in favour. (J.Scrace)

ELTHAM WELL HALL

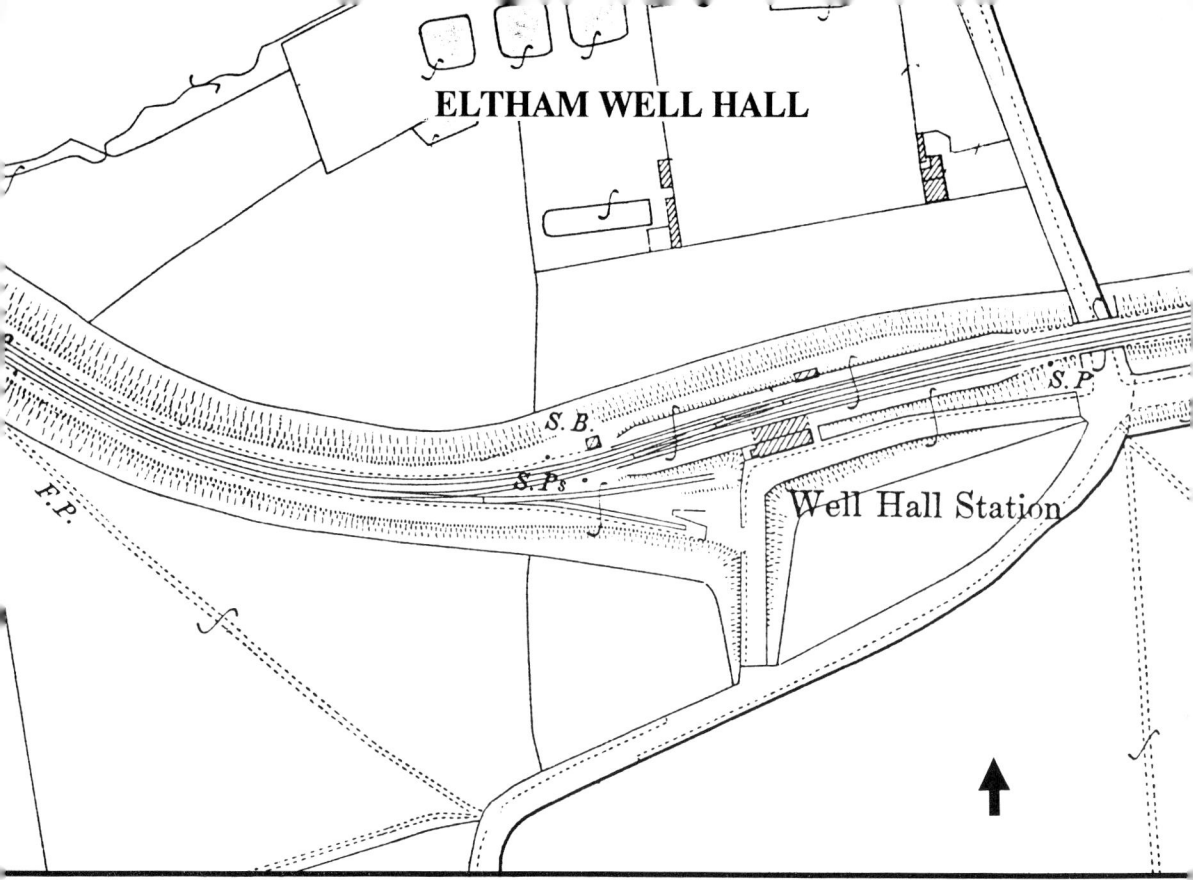

Like the other stations between Blackheath and Dartford (except Eltham Park and Falconwood), "Well Hall" opened with the line on 1st May 1895. This is the 1897 survey. The name was changed to "Well Hall and North Eltham" on 1st October 1916 and to "Eltham (Well Hall)" on 26th September 1927.

21. Probably taken within ten years of the opening, this northward view from Sherrard Road includes the small goods shed, marked on the next map. The goods yard was eventually equipped with a 5-ton crane.
(Lens of Sutton)

22. Class Q1 no.361 departs with the 2.5pm Blackheath to Erith service on 12th September 1920. At this time, only four trains ran to Dartford and all but this one originated from London termini. The population of Eltham had grown to 28,000 from 6,000 when the line opened. (K.Nunn/LCGB)

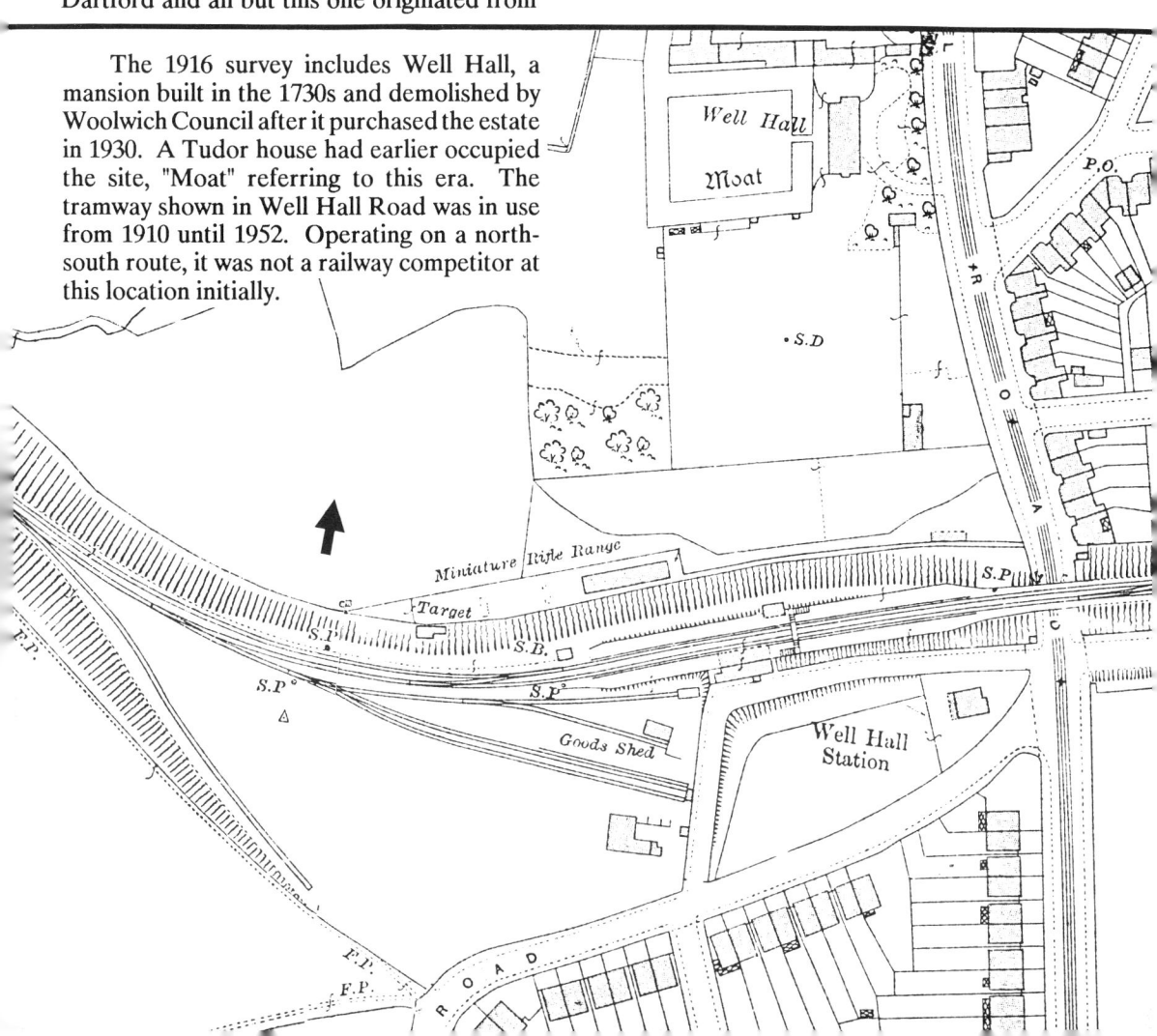

The 1916 survey includes Well Hall, a mansion built in the 1730s and demolished by Woolwich Council after it purchased the estate in 1930. A Tudor house had earlier occupied the site, "Moat" referring to this era. The tramway shown in Well Hall Road was in use from 1910 until 1952. Operating on a north-south route, it was not a railway competitor at this location initially.

23. Photographed in June 1956, the footbridge had been erected in 1907. The signal box was closed on 15th March 1970. The fourth rail was to improve current return in this vicinity. The goods yard in the distance closed on 7th October 1968. The up platform canopy was damaged during WWII and replaced about 10 years later. (British Rail)

24. EPB no. 5710 heads east in about 1958, passing the entrance to the steps to street level and the platform extension. This was added in 1955 to accommodate 10-car trains. (N.L.Browne)

25. A local freight passes through on 11th June 1961, headed by a C class locomotive. In the 1950s, the yard had been served by trains from Blackheath at about 2am and 8pm and so were unlikely to be photographed. On this route, the C class was restricted to 25 wagons down and 20 up. (A.E.Bennett)

26. An EPB is recorded at the up platform on 16th March 1985, the last day on which the station was used. Its successor is visible in the distance. Also evident are the check rails (and associated flange greasers) provided for the 12-chain curve west of the station, which was subject to a 20 mph speed limit. (C.Wilson)

27. The sharp curve resulted from the original route being projected to Lee and diverted to Blackheath. A down train has just climbed the 1 in 75 gradient on 16th March 1985 and is passing the once-convenient convenience, prior to entering the station on its last day of use. It will have passed over Westhorne Avenue, where the present 440-ton bridge was rolled into position on 29th November 1931. (C.Wilson)

ELTHAM (WELL HALL).

Loose shunting.—Loose shunting of wagons from the down to the up line at this station is strictly forbidden.

Engines running round trains or wagons at this station must under no circumstances have wagons trailing, on account of the heavy gradients.

Crossing from up line to up siding.—Owing to the curvature of the crossing from up line to up sidings, vehicles with a wheel base of 18 feet and upwards cannot be dealt with at this station.

ELTHAM

28. The new station came into use on 17th March 1985, superseding both Eltham Well Hall and Eltham Park. The 09.33 Charing Cross to Dartford service arrives on 16th June 1989. From August to November 1986, the line west of the station was moved southwards while a new bridge was built to take the tracks over the realigned A2. (S.C.Nash)

29. The new station was provided with excellent bus interchange facilities, which were built over the Rochester Way Relief Road, the A2, which is in a deep cutting. The platforms are concealed by the glass on the left. (J.Scrace)

ELTHAM PARK

30. The SECR opened this station on 1st July 1908, the buildings being designed by Sir Arthur Bloomfield & Sons and erected on a bridge over the line. The railway company had then intended to close Well Hall station, but legal problems delayed this for nearly 80 years. (Lens of Sutton)

31. Opened as "Shooters Hill and Eltham Park", the prefix was dropped on 1st October 1927. This photo appears to have been taken at the time of the opening, as the poster boards are waiting to be erected. The Well Hall distant signal bears the arrow - shaped Coligny - Welch indicator and the barrow bears an exhibitionist. (Lens of Sutton)

32. Spacious waiting rooms and long canopies were provided on both platforms making it the most opulent station on the line. The photograph was taken in May 1912, prior to the erection of the footbridge. (Lens of Sutton)

The 1916 map was published before Glenlea Road (left) was extended across Westmount Road, south of the station.

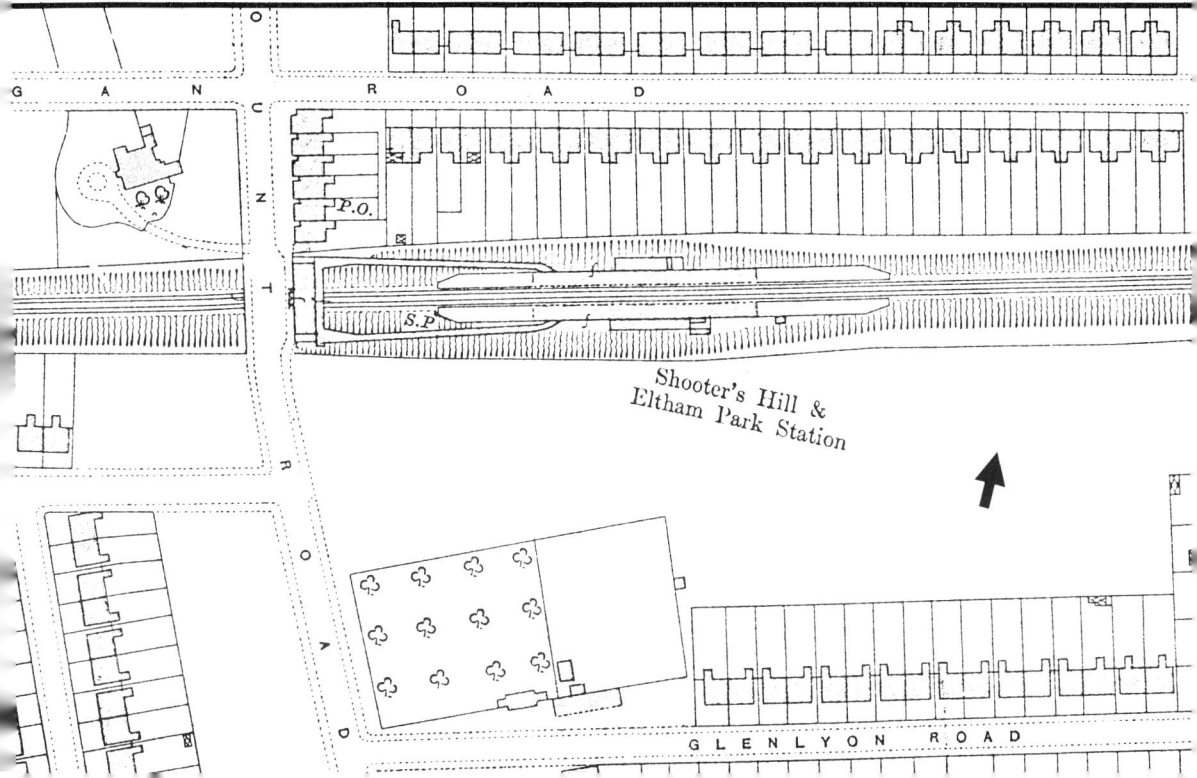

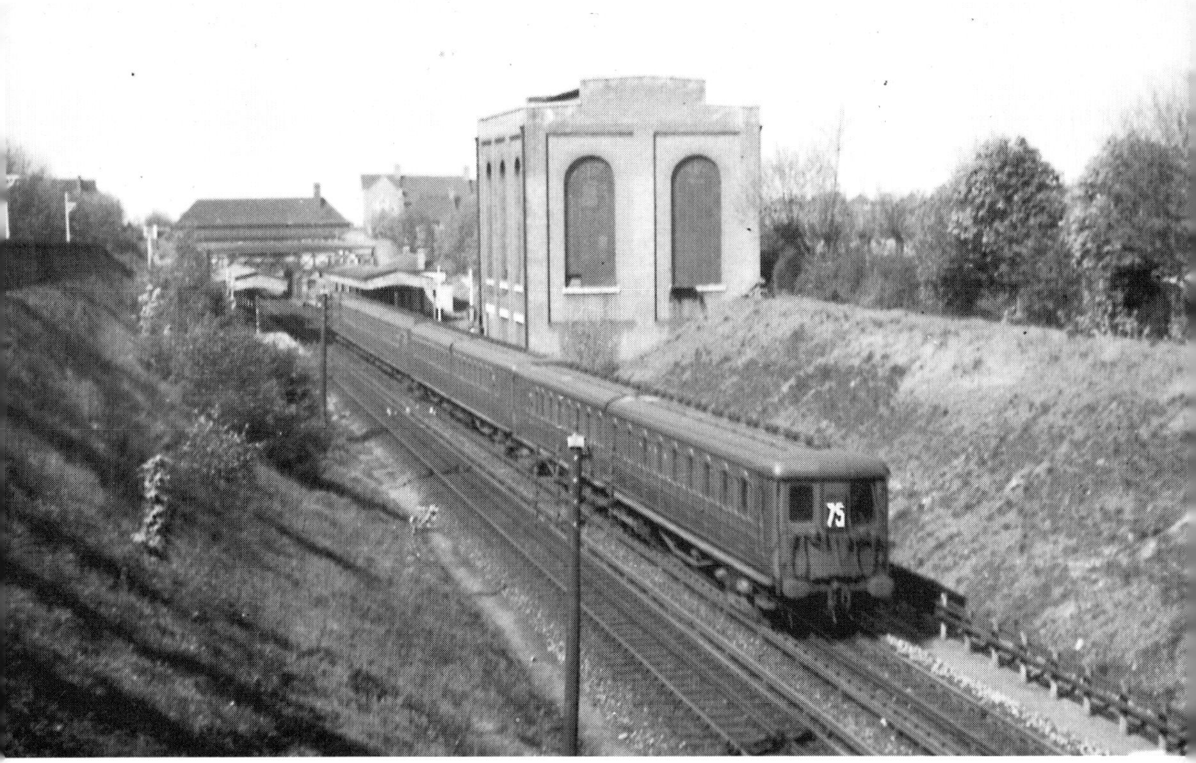
75

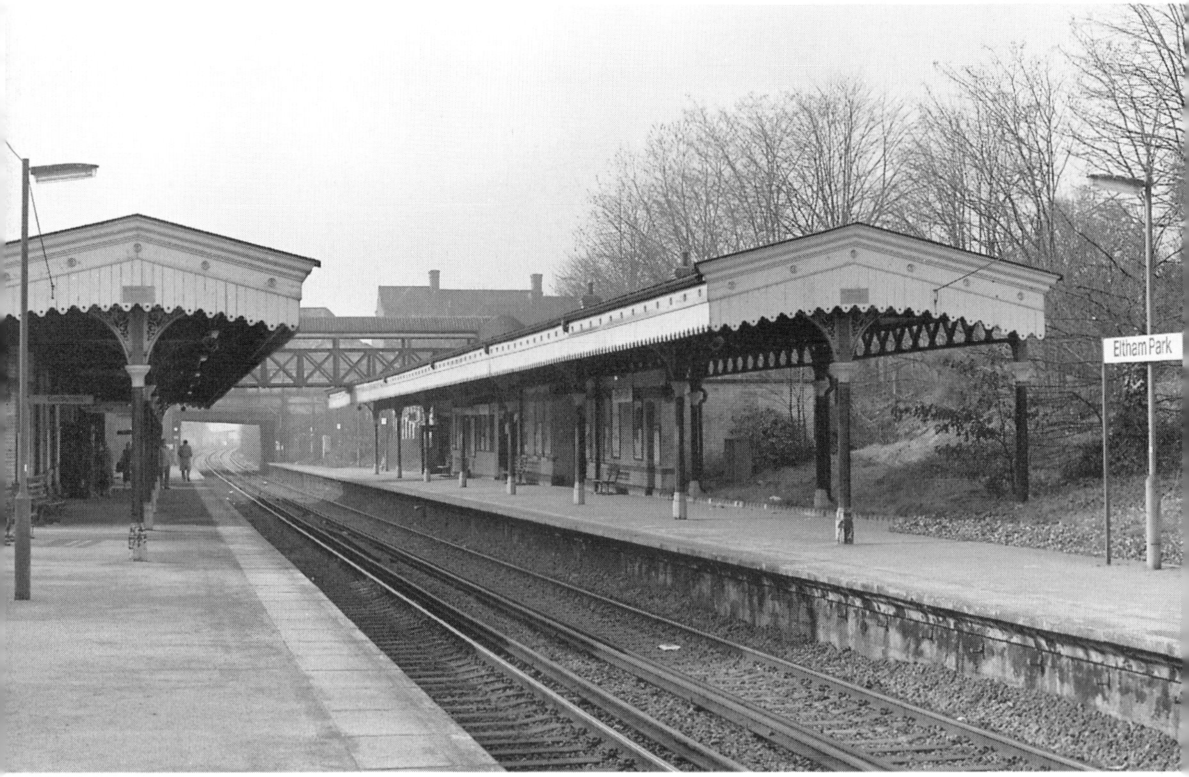
Eltham Park

33. The footbridge was added in 1924 so that the street level accommodation could be converted to shops and the booking office moved to the up platform. Eastbound passengers could thus use the bridge after purchasing their tickets. The sub-station on the right was long known as Shooters Hill. The 9.38am from Cannon Street is seen on 21st May 1949, along with the original power distribution cables and fourth rail - see picture no. 40 for details of this. Leading is ex-LSWR 2NOL no. 1852. (Dr.E.Course)

35. The class 415 (4EPBs) were introduced in 1951 and thus many served the route for over 40 years. This example is seen just prior to the station closure, when an attempt was made by the South Eastern & Chatham Railway Preservation Society to rescue the canopy components. (D.Brown)

34. The intricate cast iron stanchions are seen a few days before the scheduled closure date of 2nd March 1985. Delays in completing the new station in the distance resulted in closure being postponed until the 16th. The plinth of the buildings reveals that the platforms were on a considerable gradient - 1 in 81. (D.Brown)

FALCONWOOD

36. The station was opened by the SR on 1st January 1936, colour light signals being installed from the outset. The crossover in the background of this eastward view was added in January 1972. (J.Scrace)

37. With the advent of colour light signalling on the entire route in 1970, Falconwood became the boundary between the two controlling panels situated at Dartford and London Bridge. There is evidence of platform lengthening at the London end. (J.Scrace)

38. Opened in response to local speculative building activity, the main building (on the left of the previous picture) retains its classical SR style, although the booking office was modernised internally in 1978. All three photographs were taken in March 1990. (J.Scrace)

Network South East   Falconwood

WELLING

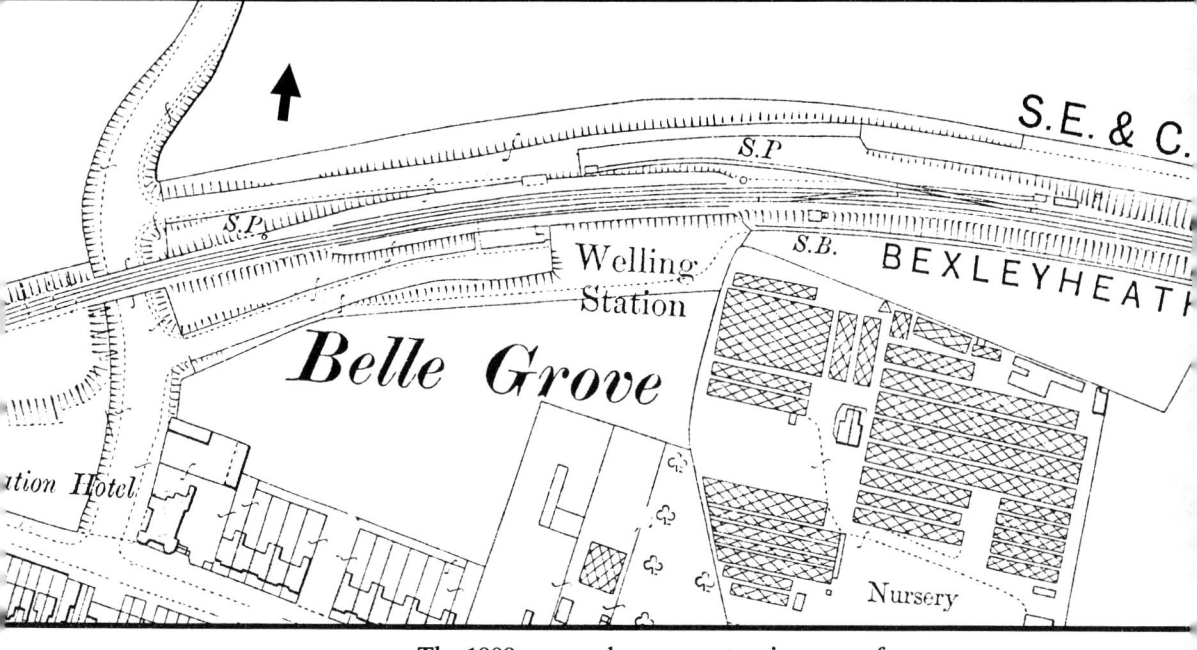

The 1909 survey shows an extensive area of glasshouses close to the station and open fields to the north.

39. Opened with the line, a standard set of buildings was provided, along with a loading gauge, visible in the distance. The sash window is wide open on 30th September 1923, as an up train arrives. Plans for a new station were drawn up in 1931.
(H.J.Patterson-Rutherford)

40. There is evidence of platform lengthening at both ends, when they were photographed on 29th June 1954. The fourth rails were to increase return current capacity, as a high amperage could flow when trains were climbing up the 1 in 89 gradient from the east. Note the bonding cable in the foreground. (British Rail)

The 1936 edition indicates complete urban development within the environs of the station and an extra coal siding to meet the requirements of the increased number of hearths. The yard closed on 3rd December 1962.

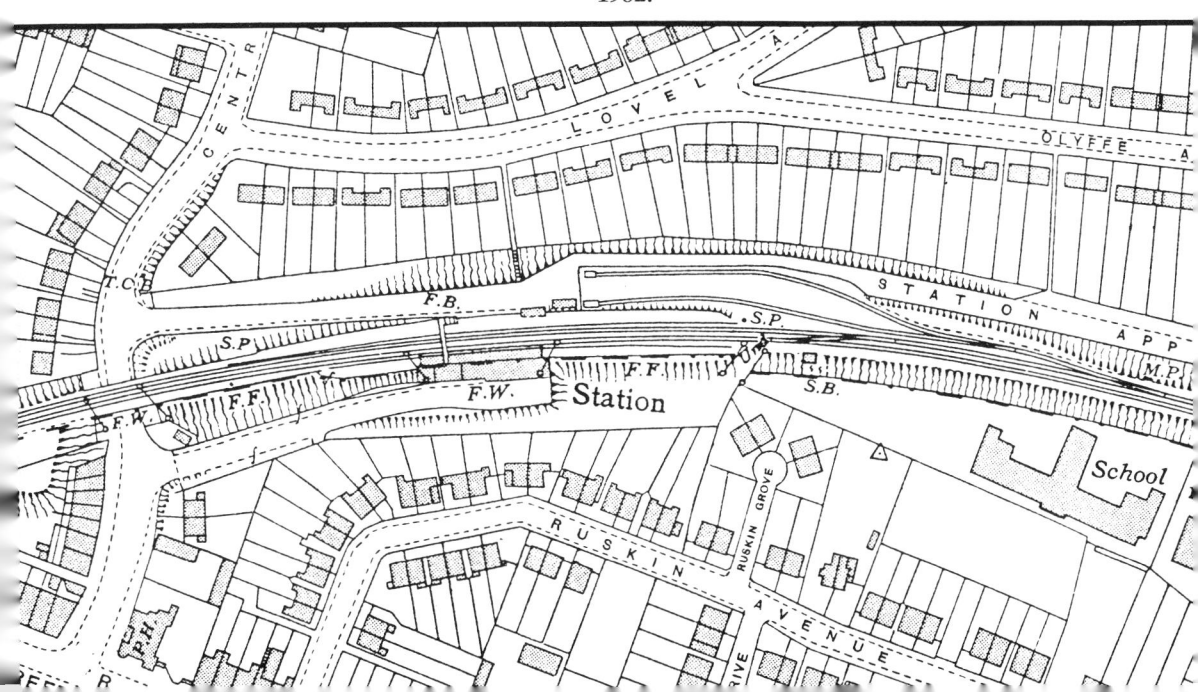

41. The 14.49 Dartford to Charing Cross, on 5th June 1969, passes the site of the former goods yard (left) and the signal box, which closed on 1st November 1970. (J.Scrace)

(below)
42. The main buildings are on the up side and are seen from a private rooftop carpark on 31st March 1990. (J.Scrace)

(lower right)
43. Another photograph from the same day shows the 11.33 Charing Cross to Dartford service. In 1991 the platforms were further lengthened at their east end in readiness for the 12-car Networker class 465 trains. (J.Scrace)

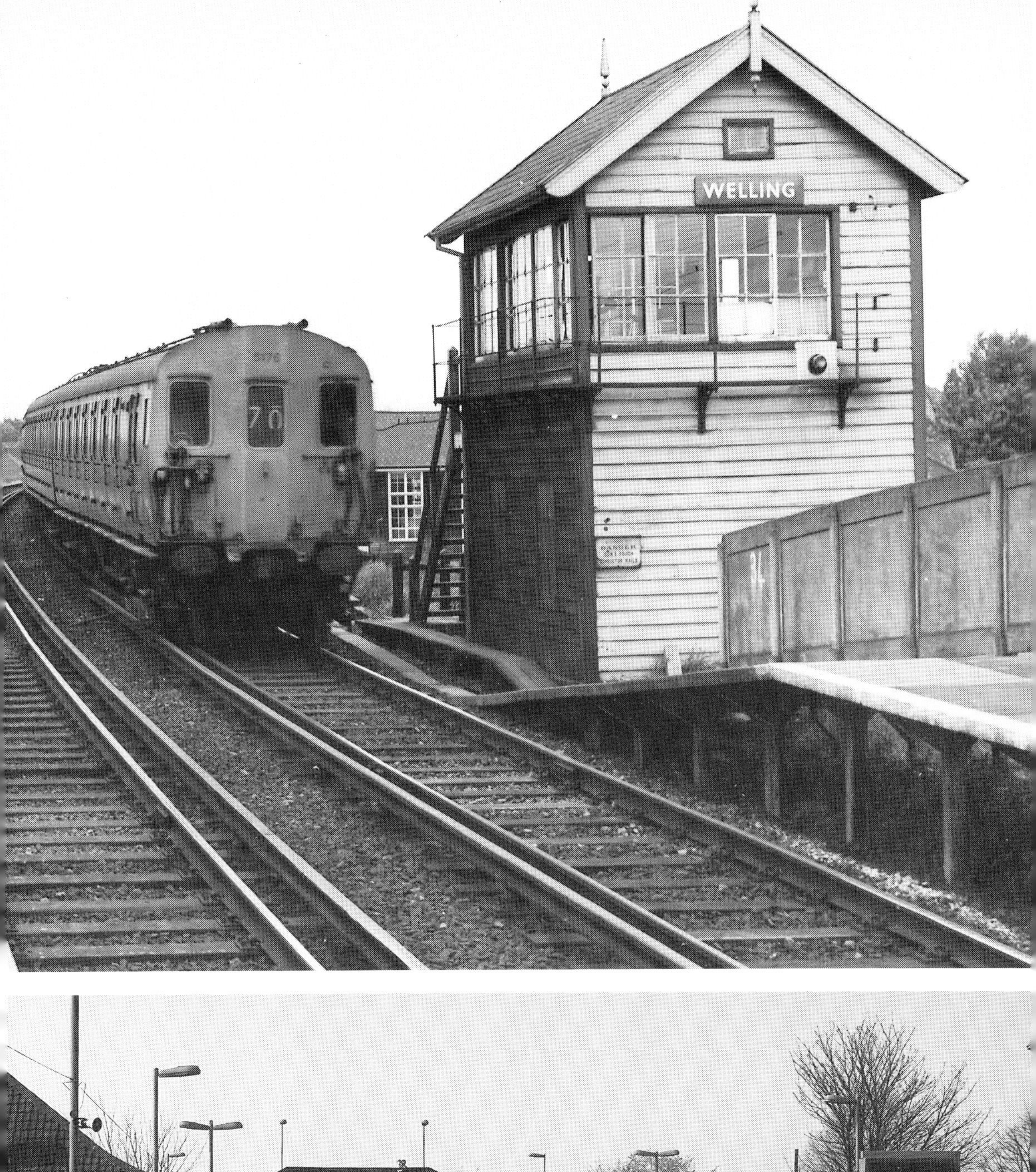
WELLING
70

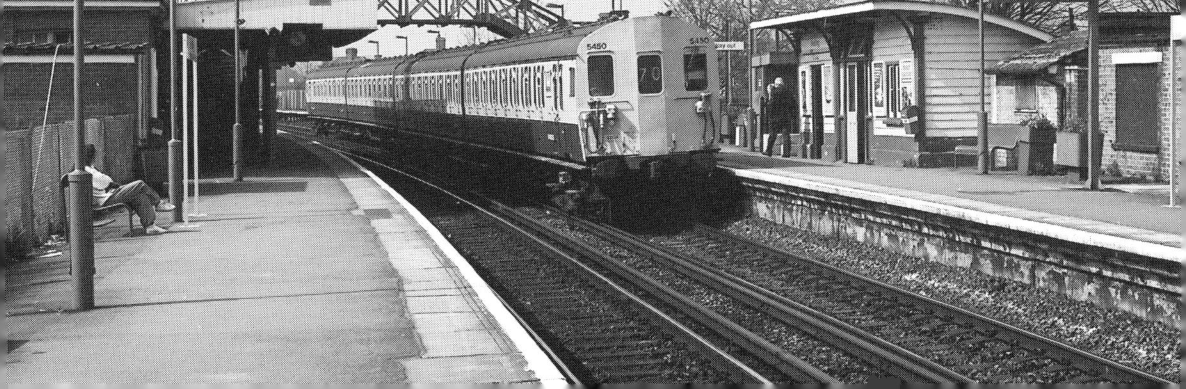
5450
5450
70

BEXLEYHEATH

44. A pre-electrification eastward view shows a crossover under the road bridge and the standard SER wooden building. The small signal box is visible at the end of the up platform. (H.J.Patterson-Rutherford)

45. The goods yard mainly handled coal and is seen on 31st May 1959 as the 10.35am van train from Ramsgate to Holborn Viaduct passes, hauled by class E1 no.31497. The yard closed on 7th October 1968. (J.J.Smith)

The 1908 map reveals that the goods yard was remote from the station, as the latter was located in a cutting. Little housing development had taken place at that time.

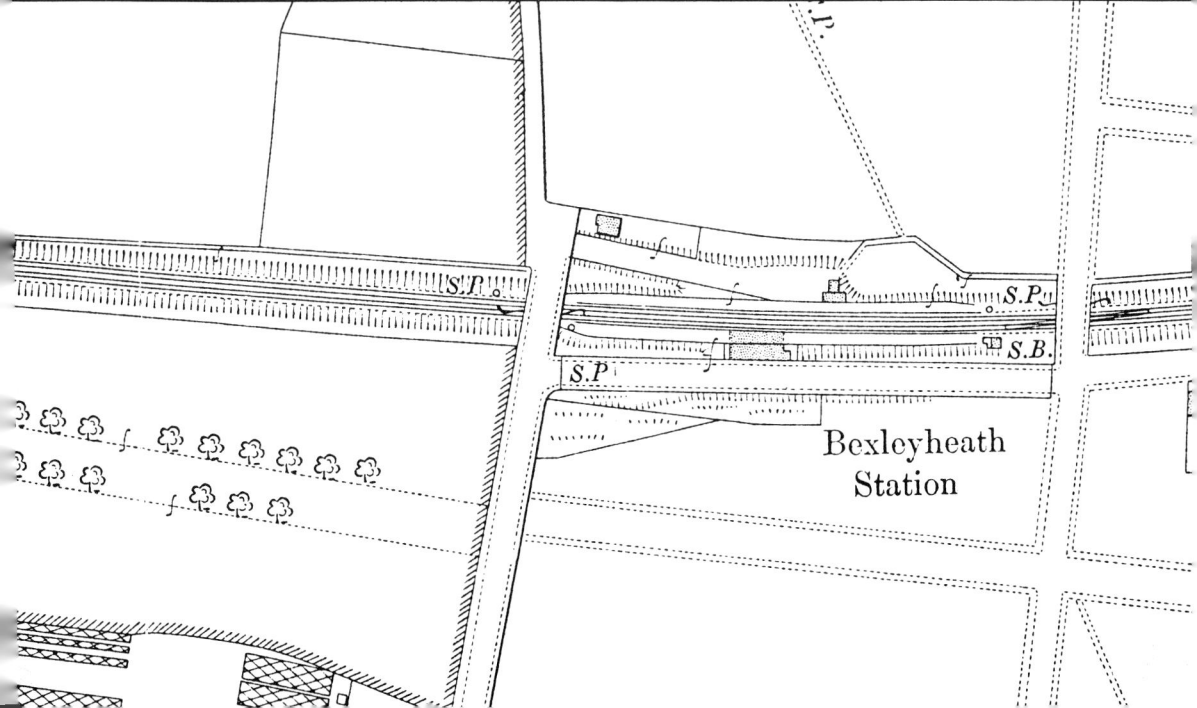

Bexleyheath Station

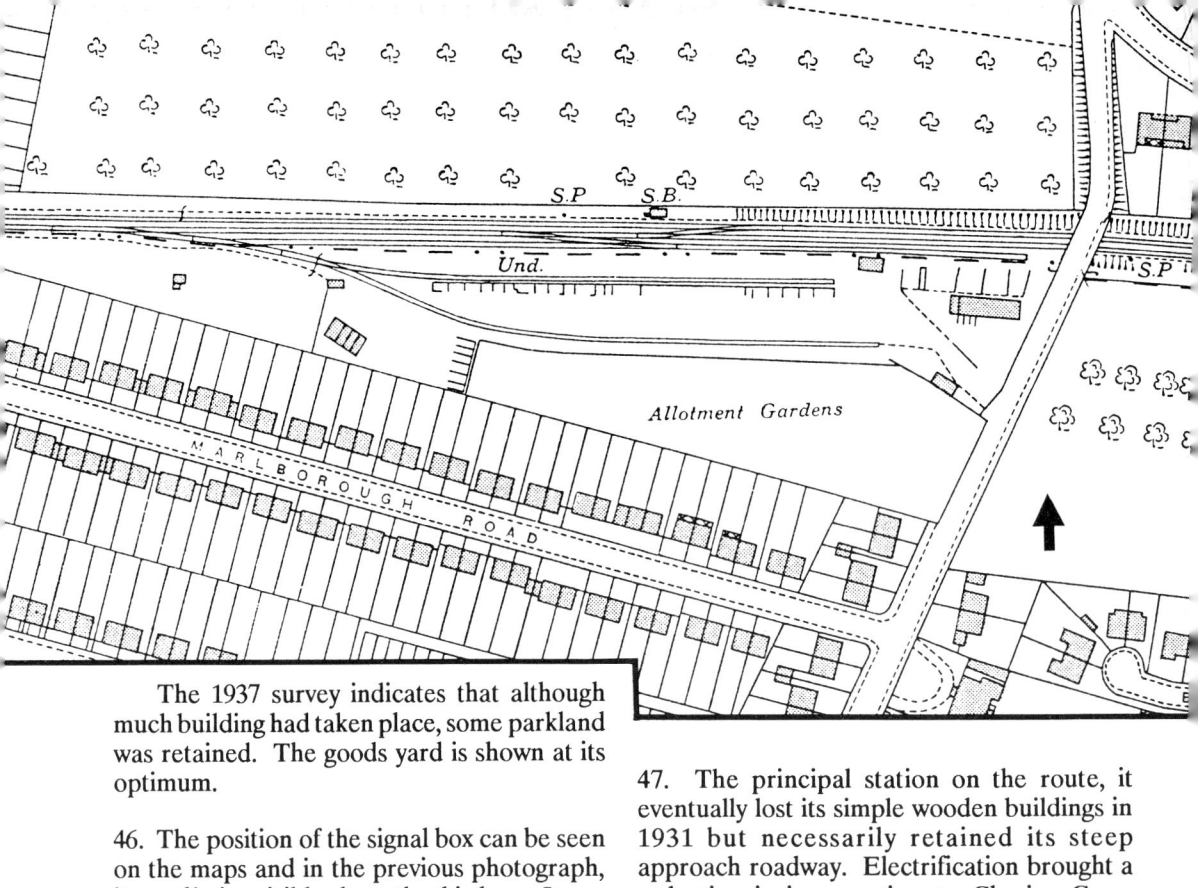

The 1937 survey indicates that although much building had taken place, some parkland was retained. The goods yard is shown at its optimum.

46. The position of the signal box can be seen on the maps and in the previous photograph, its roof being visible above the third van. It was taken out of use on 1st November 1970 and is seen in 1968. (J.Scrace)

47. The principal station on the route, it eventually lost its simple wooden buildings in 1931 but necessarily retained its steep approach roadway. Electrification brought a reduction in journey time to Charing Cross from 51 to 34 minutes and then house building boomed. (J.Scrace)

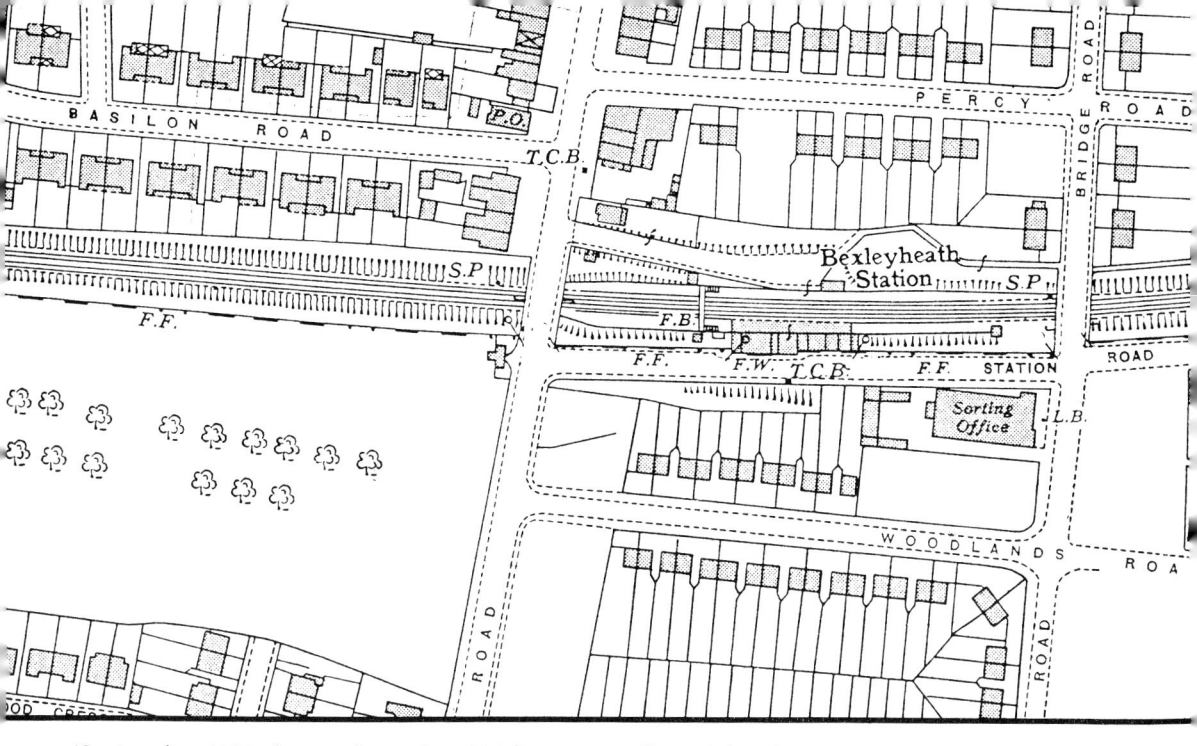

48. Another 1990 picture shows the 1924 footbridge and the main buildings, which are on the up side, as at other stations on the route. The spelling of Bexleyheath as one word was confirmed by the local council in the year before the line opened but the railway was slow to conform. (J.Scrace)

BARNEHURST

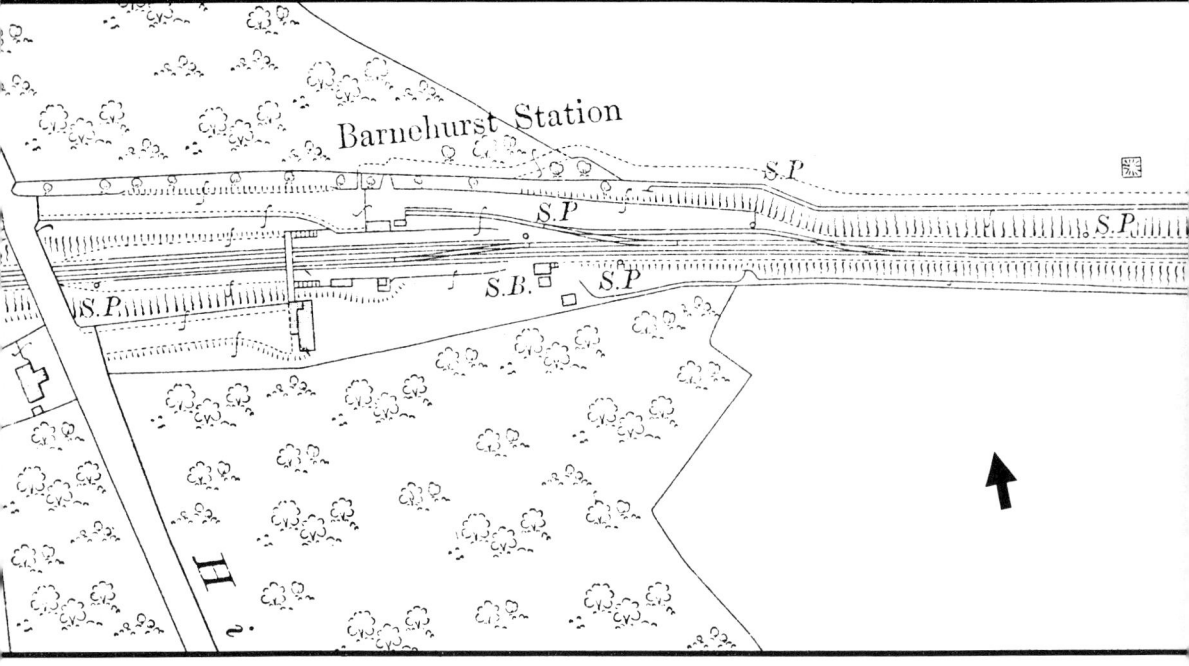

The name was derived from the woodland belonging to Colonel Barne in which the station was built. The 1909 edition marks a single siding which had an end loading dock, presumably for the benefit of the Colonel, who was a director of the railway.

49. Barnehurst was unusual on the route in having its wooden building (right) remote from, and at a right angle to, the track and in having a footbridge from the outset. This eastward view is from 1923.
(H.J.Patterson-Rutherford)

50. A photograph from June 1954 shows the recently completed platform extensions for 10-car trains and the two sidings of the coal yard. The crossover was still in place in 1991. (British Rail)

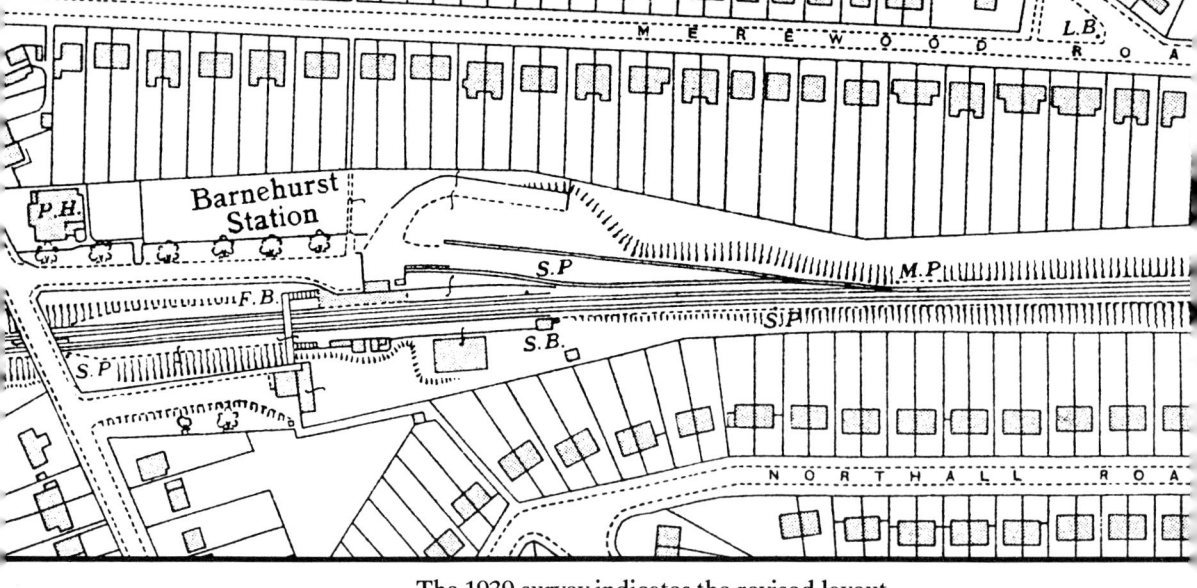

The 1939 survey indicates the revised layout
of the goods yard and the replacement of trees
by dwellings.

51. The line, at this point, is on a gradient of 1 in 75 up towards London. Prior to the advent of continuous train brakes, approval would not have been given for a station on this gradient. (British Rail)

52. Pictured in 1968, the signal box ceased to function on 1st November 1970. Beyond it is the sub-station building which originally housed rotary converters producing 660 volts DC for the conductor rail from 3300 volts AC, supplied from "Deptford Power House". (J.N.Faulkner)

53. Perry Street Fork Junction is 1½ miles east of Barnehurst and is the point of divergence of the lines to Slade Green (right) and Dartford (foreground). The box closed on 1st November 1970 and was photographed two months earlier. Perry Street is a locality, not a highway. (J.Scrace)

55. On 8th April 1991, the new depot was officially opened, a mock-up of a class 465 driving coach being shown alongside one of its predecessors, repainted in the original green livery. The new all aluminium units are fitted with lavatories with waste holding tanks and so the depot has had to be equipped with special emptying facilities. (British Rail)

Other views of the depot can be seen in pictures nos. 108 to 112 in our *Charing Cross to Dartford* **album.**

SLADE GREEN DEPOT

54. Trains from Bexleyheath to Dartford pass the southern part of the depot, where a repair shed had been built in 1925, for the maintenance of electric stock. The shed to the north had been erected in 1901 to house 110 steam locomotives and later adapted as a carriage shed for EMUs. The maintenance depot was rebuilt in 1990-91 in readiness for the third generation electric trains - the class 465, which has 1044 seats in a 12-coach train. (British Rail)

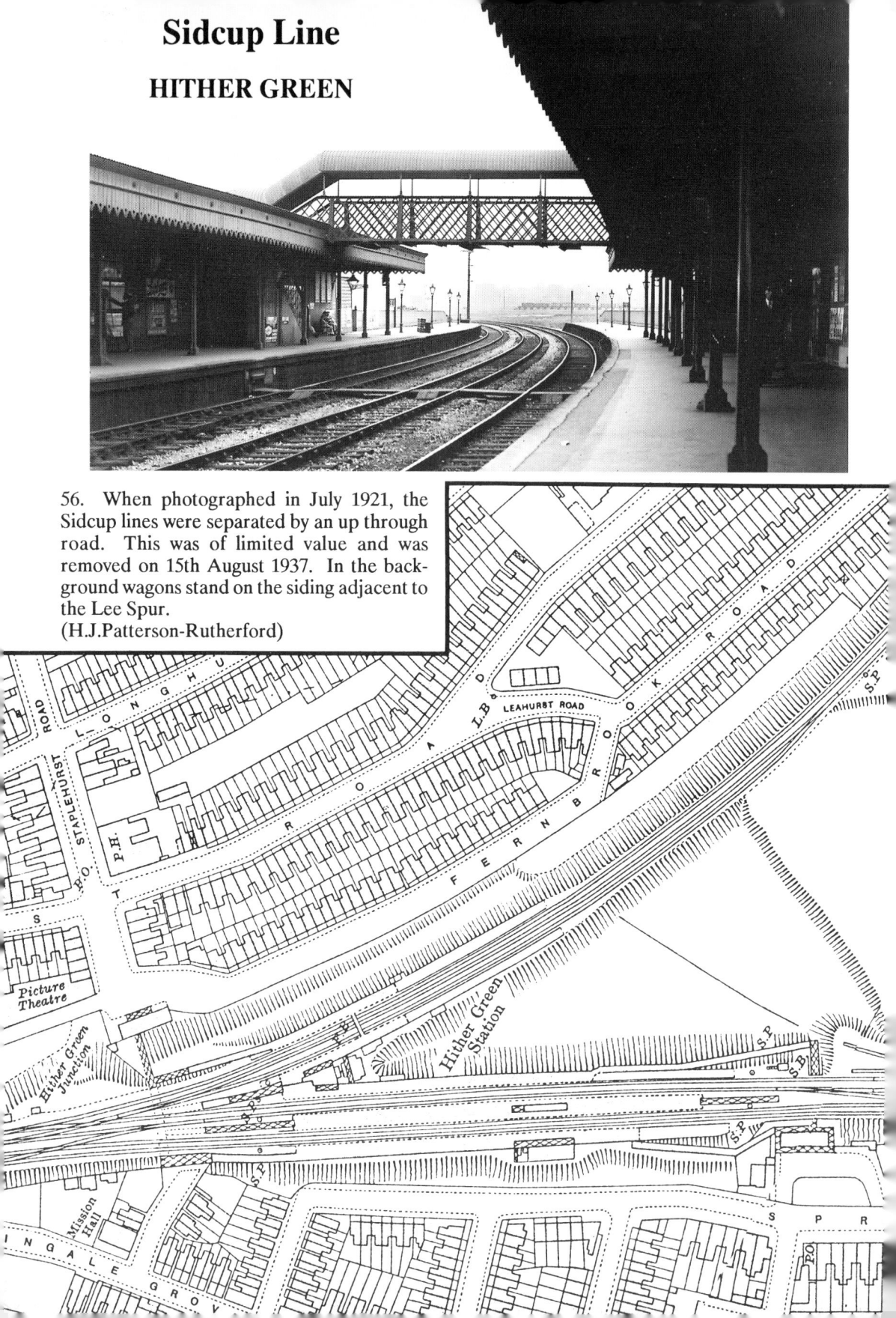

Sidcup Line

HITHER GREEN

56. When photographed in July 1921, the Sidcup lines were separated by an up through road. This was of limited value and was removed on 15th August 1937. In the background wagons stand on the siding adjacent to the Lee Spur.
(H.J.Patterson-Rutherford)

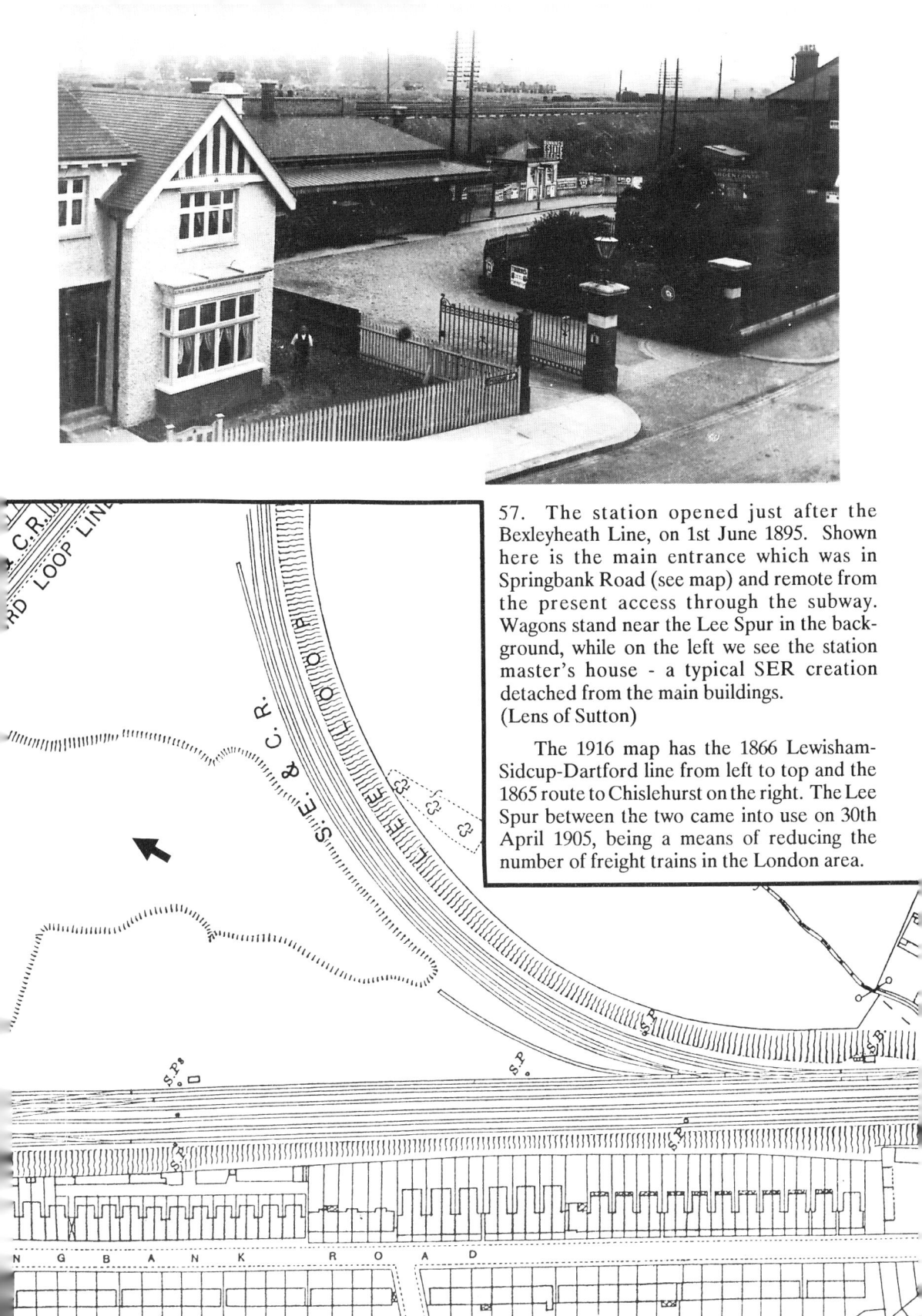

57. The station opened just after the Bexleyheath Line, on 1st June 1895. Shown here is the main entrance which was in Springbank Road (see map) and remote from the present access through the subway. Wagons stand near the Lee Spur in the background, while on the left we see the station master's house - a typical SER creation detached from the main buildings.
(Lens of Sutton)

The 1916 map has the 1866 Lewisham-Sidcup-Dartford line from left to top and the 1865 route to Chislehurst on the right. The Lee Spur between the two came into use on 30th April 1905, being a means of reducing the number of freight trains in the London area.

58. Quadrupling of the main line to Orpington took place in 1903-04, the roof on the right covering the steps to the new island platform. Hither Green Station "A" Box stands by the junction with the Sidcup Line, in this 1938 view. The colour light signals were added in 1929, at the time of the opening of the Lewisham Loop Lines. (H.N.James)

59. The same signal box is visible as C class no.31054 heads an up freight from the Sidcup Line on 3rd March 1957. Most goods trains from this route terminated at Hither Green but some ran to Bricklayers Arms, Herne Hill, Clapham Junction or Willesden.
(A.E.Bennett)

60. An 8-car double deck train was introduced in 1949 in an attempt to reduce overcrowding but its loading time was so great that it caused delays. The two sets are seen in platform 5 on 18th May 1957, by which time 10-coach trains were provided instead. The headcode indicates Crayford to Charing Cross. (J.N.Faulkner)

61. Bearing the Kent Link symbol by the leading compartment, unit no. 5619 leaves the main line on 25th April 1990. The dreary asbestos cladding dates from modernisation work in 1972. The booking office and toilets are now located in the angle between platforms 4 and 5. (J.Scrace)

62. Five class 60s have recently been allocated to Hither Green to take over duties of the class 33s, which often worked in pairs. No. 60017 *Arenig Fawr* leaves the main line on 21st May 1991, hauling empty wagons from Purley to Cliffe. (B.Morrison)

EAST OF HITHER GREEN

63. The 12.38pm Dartford to Charing Cross was hauled by class F no. 210 on 14th April 1923. It is passing Lee Junction Box, the Lee Spur being to the right of it. The box remained in use until 4th February 1962. (K.Nunn/LCGB)

64. Running north on the Lee Spur on 12th March 1960 is class 71 no. E5010, one of the batch of 13 electric locomotives built for the Kent Coast electrification scheme and fitted with pantographs for use in certain sidings. They were subsequently converted to electro-diesels. Above the first wagon is the roof of Hither Green Sidings "A" Box. (J.N.Faulkner)

LEE

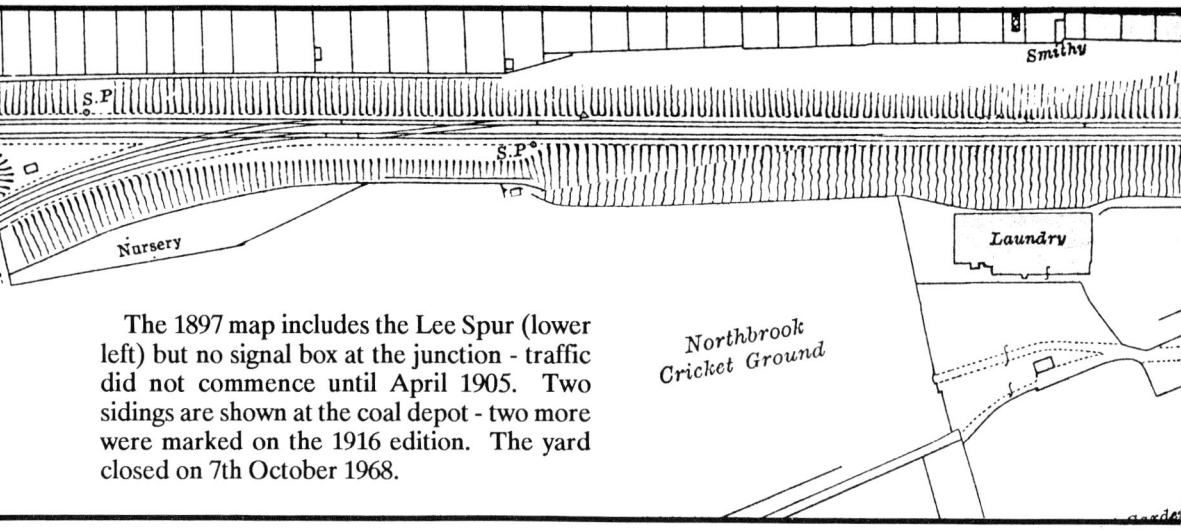

The 1897 map includes the Lee Spur (lower left) but no signal box at the junction - traffic did not commence until April 1905. Two sidings are shown at the coal depot - two more were marked on the 1916 edition. The yard closed on 7th October 1968.

65. Seen in the 1950s, the main buildings were on the up side, at the top of a steep driveway from Burnt Ash Hill. A station master's house was built in 1872, when other station improvements were made. (Lens of Sutton)

66. A westward view in 1967 from the up platform reveals the differing designs of the canopies. Part of the valance on the up side is missing, to improve signal sighting. The population of Lee grew from about 6000 to 16000 in the first 30 years of the railway. (J.N.Faulkner)

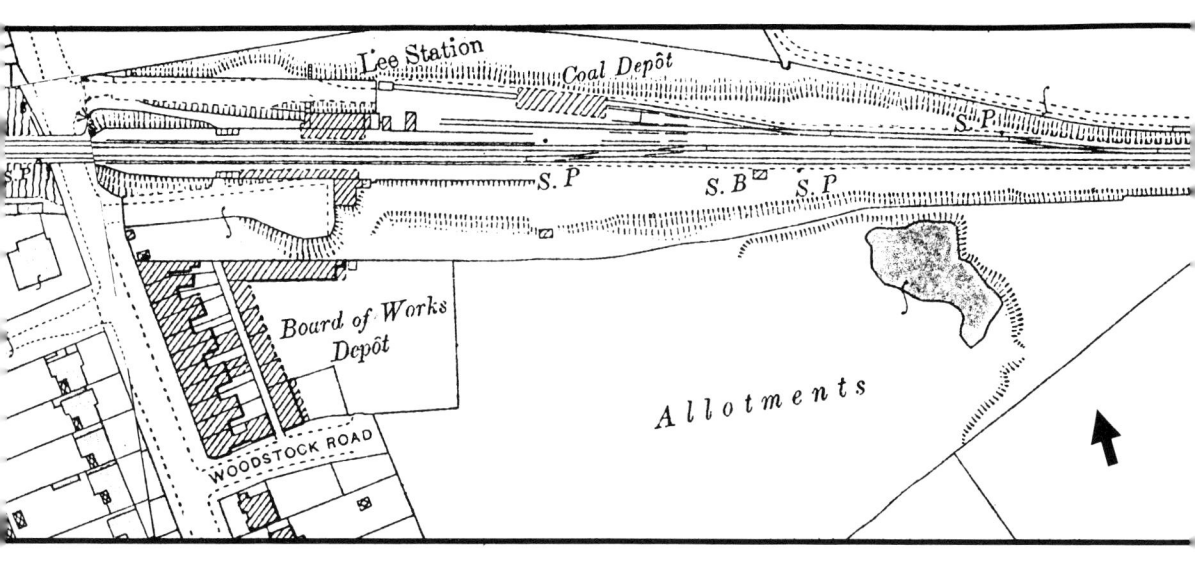

67. Lee Junction signal is visible as no. 33001 runs east with the 16.15 Dundee to Dover Speedlink service on 2nd April 1985. Speedlink wagon-load facilities were withdrawn nationally in July 1991, only weeks after the government demanded that rail freight should be doubled and only two years before every siding in Britain would be directly connected with the rest of Europe. (J.S.Petley)

68. No. 56004, one of a batch of diesel-electrics built in Romania, approaches Lee on 23rd October 1986, with an MGR coal train from Toton to Northfleet Cement Works. Lee becomes particularly busy when Victoria-Kent Coast services are diverted, fast trains stopping here to connect with a special bus link to Bromley South. (D.Brown)

69. Looking east in 1988, we can see the position of the subway steps, not revealed in the other pictures. The down side buildings were rebuilt in 1991. (J.Scrace)

70. A 1990 photograph of the 1988 up side accommodation features the transparent waiting room/booking hall, undoubtedly a brighter environment for intending passengers, by then redesignated non-specifically as customers. (J.Scrace)

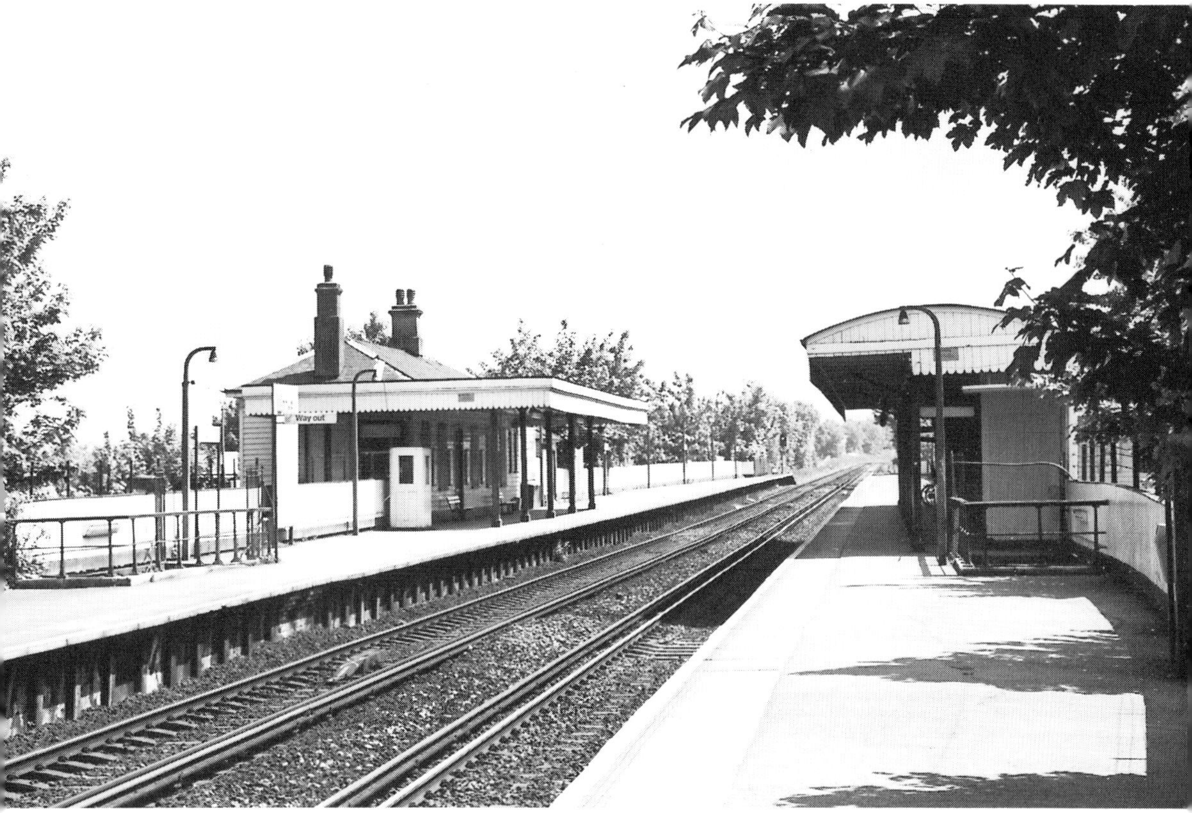
Way out

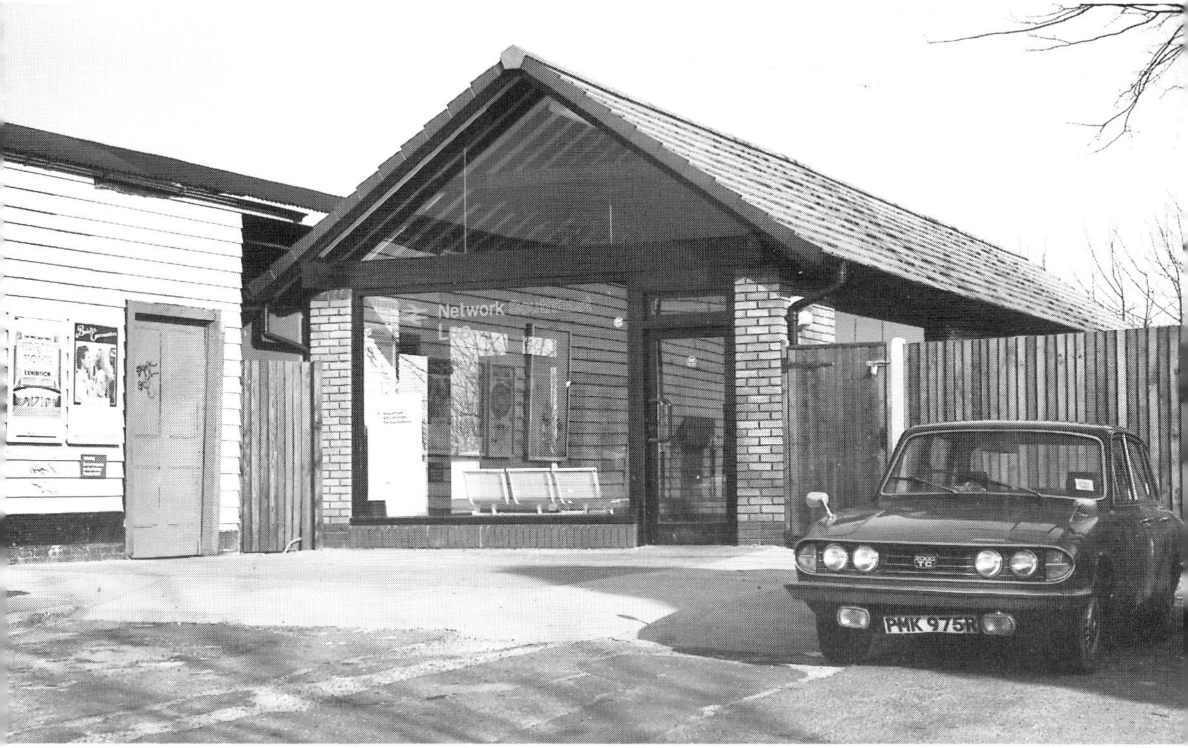
Network
EXHIBITION
PMK 975R

EAST OF LEE

71. No. 73136 hauls tankers from the Rugby Portland Cement terminal at Southampton to Halling Cement Works on 9th June 1984. This was an unusual working for a Saturday but typifies the variety of freight services to use the route. (J.S.Petley)

72. On 11th October 1977, the derailed wagons of an eastbound coal train were struck by a Northfleet to Dunstable cement train, hauled by two class 33s. No. 33036 is seen at the bottom of a Mottingham garden in which there were several fatalities amongst caged budgerigars. (B.Morrison)

MOTTINGHAM

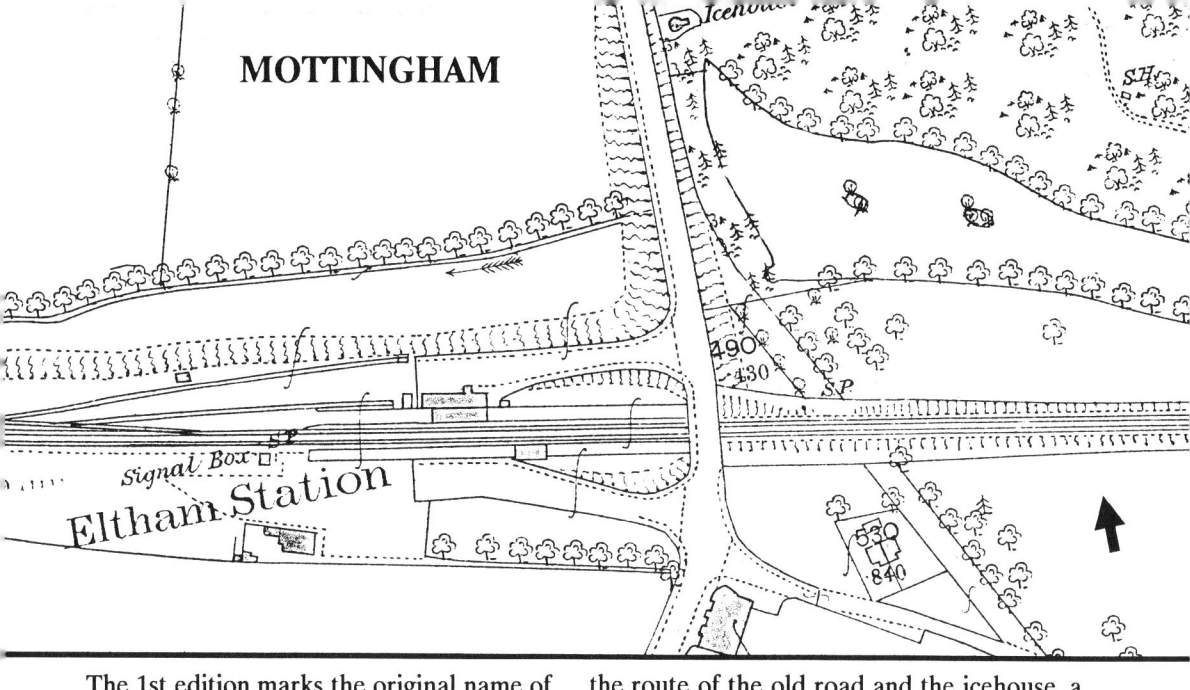

The 1st edition marks the original name of the station, which was changed to that shown on the next map on 1st January 1892. Look for

73. The station opened with the line but the population grew only slowly in response to the arrival of the railway in 1866, the rounded figures being 130 in 1861, 1,000 in 1891 and the route of the old road and the icehouse, a feature of many country estates in the pre-refrigeration era.

1,800 in 1921. This is a westward view from the road bridge. The footbridge was erected prior to 1899. (Lens of Sutton)

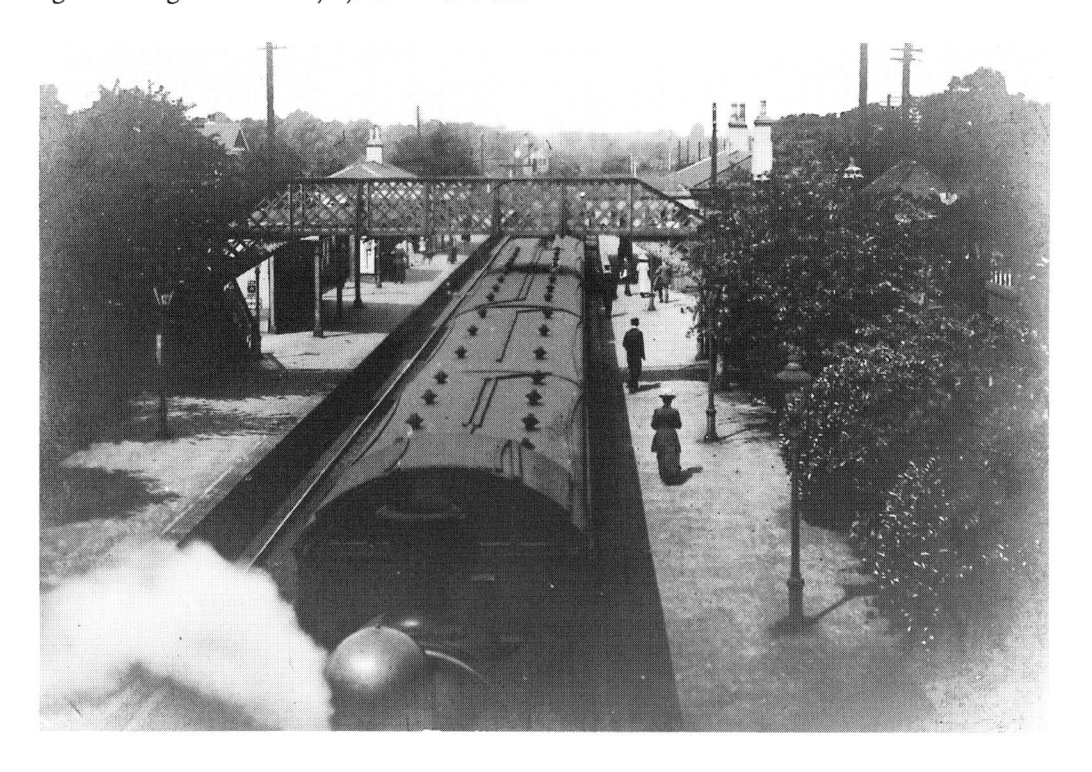

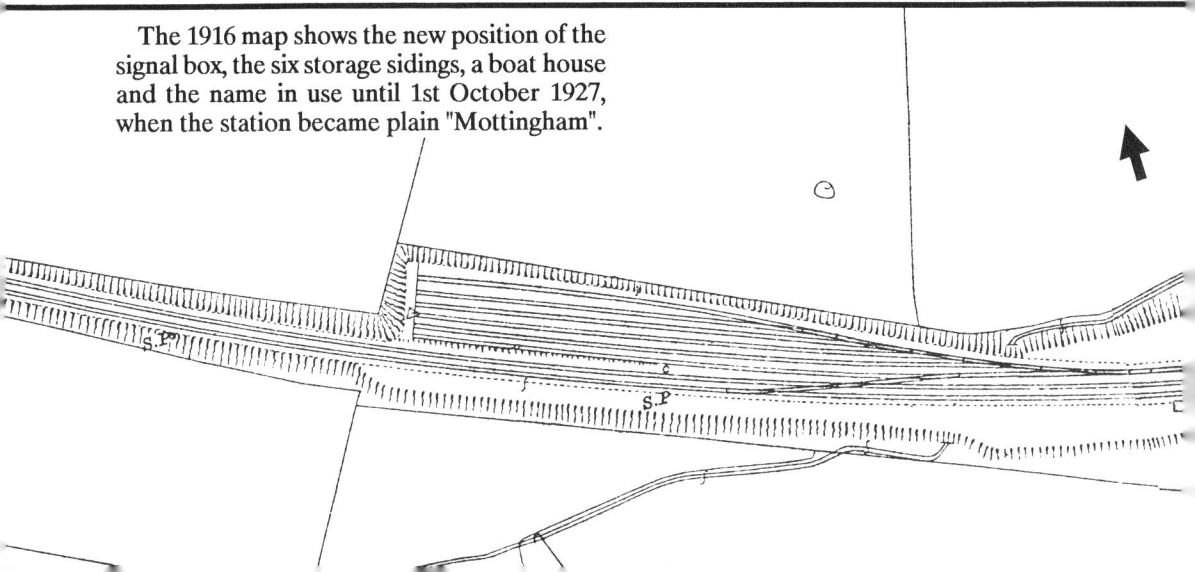

The 1916 map shows the new position of the signal box, the six storage sidings, a boat house and the name in use until 1st October 1927, when the station became plain "Mottingham".

74. On 5th June 1969, the 11.48 Charing Cross to Dartford service passes the signal box which closed on 14th September of that year and the goods yard, which had closed on 7th October of the previous year. The siding in the foreground had been used for milk traffic for many years. (J.Scrace)

75. Two 1990 pictures reveal that much of the SER weather boarding survived. Trees are evident here and for most of the length of the route, remarkable for such an urbanised area. The sign 9.. indicates 9½ miles from Charing Cross. (J.Scrace)

76. The main entrance and booking office is on the up side, as is common on both routes. The chimney in this and the previous picture marks the boundary between the old and the 1957 buildings. Mottingham is the boundary between the signalling panels at London Bridge and Dartford. (J.Scrace)

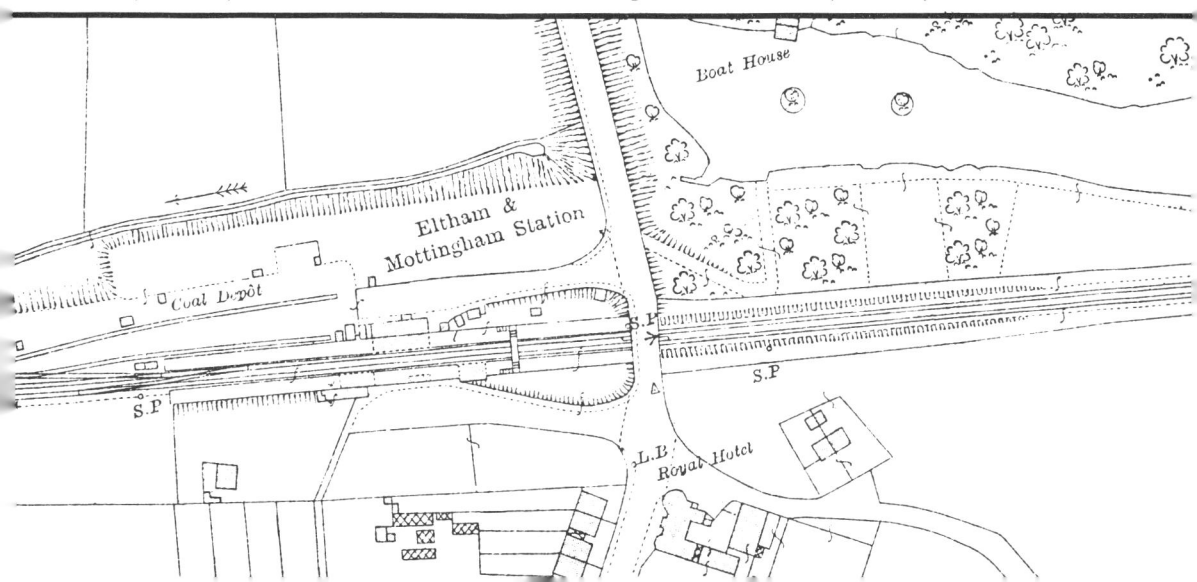

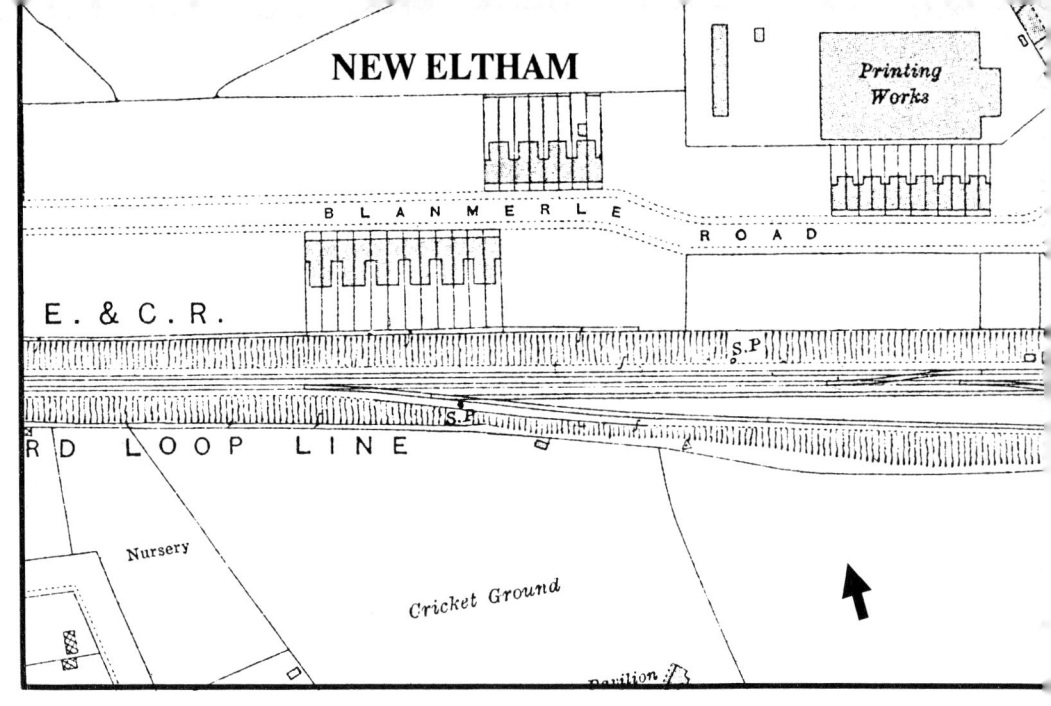

77. Opened as "Pope Street" on 1st April 1878, this station received the name shown on 1st January 1886, the suffix being officially dropped on 1st October 1927. A down train enters the well groomed station as a hay cart leaves the goods yard. (Lens of Sutton)

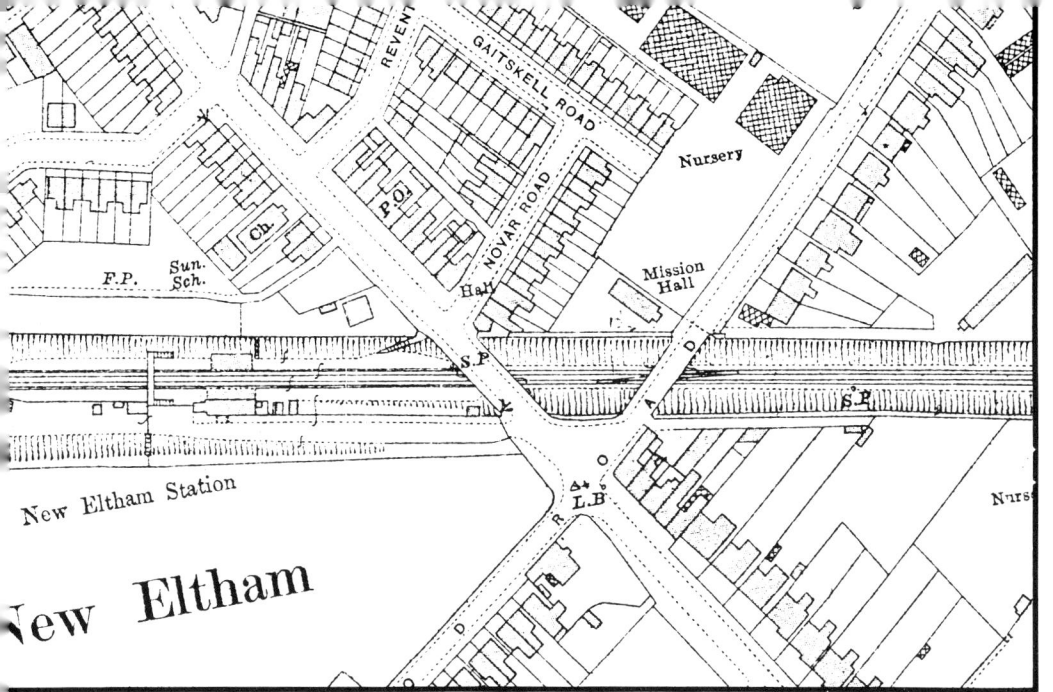

The 1916 edition has the position of the two crossovers, the steps from the down platform to street level and the end-loading dock, a facility provided at few of the stations on either route.

78. Looking towards London from the footbridge in July 1954, we see almost the full extent of the goods yard which was expensively created in a cutting and which closed on 15th May 1963. The signal box lasted until 15th May 1955. (B.Nunns/A.Mott coll.)

79. Three photographs from 11th May 1955 include work in progress to lengthen the platforms for 10-car trains. The signal box is about to be demolished to allow the extension of the down platform. (D.Cullum)

80. Other improvements at this time included replacement of the gaslights, the new concrete posts standing ready for electric wiring. The bridges carry Footscray Road and Avery Hill Road. (D.Cullum)

81. For generations, the coal order office was a familiar part of the approach to many suburban stations. In the distance a new colour light signal stands at the end of the platform extension while its semaphore predecessor is still in use. (D.Cullum)

82. Another type of locomotive to be introduced to the route in recent years is the class 59, built in the USA by General Motors for quarry owners ARC. No. 59101 is heading the Allington to Stoke Gifford service on 21st May 1991. (B.Morrison)

83. The recently rebuilt up side (right) has been given some character with canopy vaulting of Victorian style, an original example of which survives over part of the down platform at Worthing. Some rebuilding took place in 1964-65. (J.Scrace)

84. The building harmonises well with its surroundings, in particular with the lattice footbridge. This and the previous picture were taken on 22nd February 1990, when one of the posters was announcing the closure of Holborn Viaduct station. (J.Scrace)

SIDCUP

85. The station was opened in October 1866, a few days after the line, and a new booking office was built in 1887. The train includes a "Birdcage" look out and the track is ballasted over the sleepers, a technique that could conceal rotten timber. (Lens of Sutton)

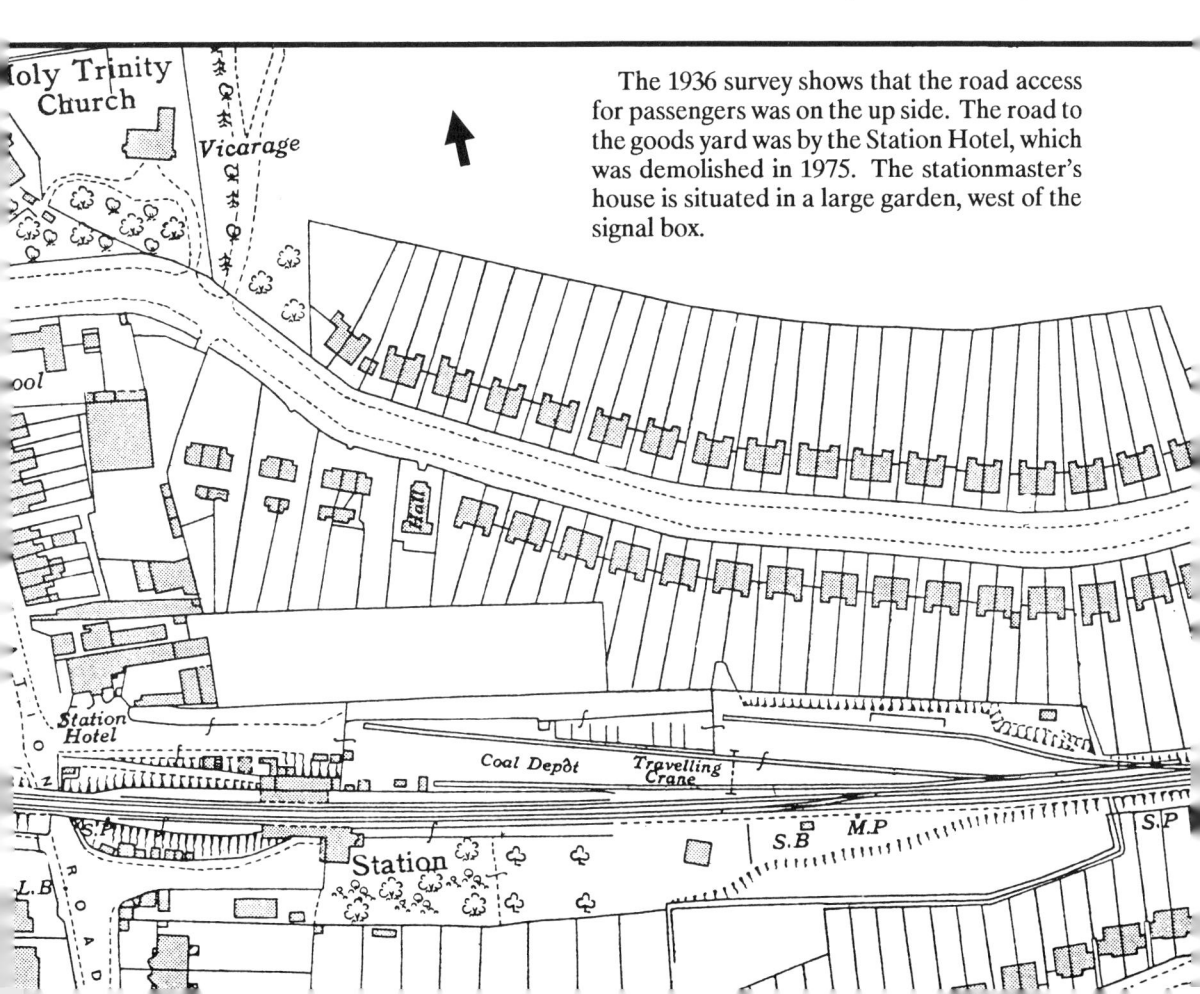

The 1936 survey shows that the road access for passengers was on the up side. The road to the goods yard was by the Station Hotel, which was demolished in 1975. The stationmaster's house is situated in a large garden, west of the signal box.

86. Not uncommon was the differing design of canopies on opposite platforms. This was due to the fact that they were built at different times and standards change. Railway managers have for long yearned for standardisation, even if local clashes result. (Lens of Sutton)

87. An eastward view in April 1953 includes the 1937 SR-style canopies and hexagonal gas lamp shades, along with the travelling crane, which was of 5-ton capacity. The yard closed on 15th August 1966. (D.Cullum)

88. The signal box is in the background of the previous picture and was in use until 1st November 1970. A conductor rail supply isolating switch is in the foreground of this 1969 picture. Just prior to this date, an electrified siding was added on the down side, to facilitate the termination of peak hour trains. (J.Scrace)

89. This 1988 view towards London was taken at the time of the reconstruction of the up side buildings. The station was built one mile north of Sidcup, in the parish of Lamorbey. The addition of a footbridge in 1965 allowed the closure of the down side booking office. (F.Hornby)

90. The imposing up side buildings had been mutilated by vandals and so this 1990 picture has been touched-up to avoid publishing their pathetic markings. The £700,000 structure was officially opened by the Deputy Mayor of Bexley on 24th November 1988. (J.Scrace)

91. The headboard announces the significance of this train on 8th November 1990. Concrete segment casting commenced on the Isle of Grain early in 1988, trains conveying them to Sevington, near Ashford, via Dartford and the Lee Spur. Pictures 82 to 85 in our *Branch Line to Allhallows* tell more of this unusual story. The locomotives are nos. 33021 and 33051. (J.Scrace)

ALBANY PARK

92. The SR opened the station on 7th July 1935, the exterior being seen soon after completion. The area was a new development, rather than the extension of an existing one. (British Rail)

The 1936 edition reveals that "semis" predominate but that monotonous parallel roads were avoided. Even the station building was placed at an angle to the railway and to the shops.

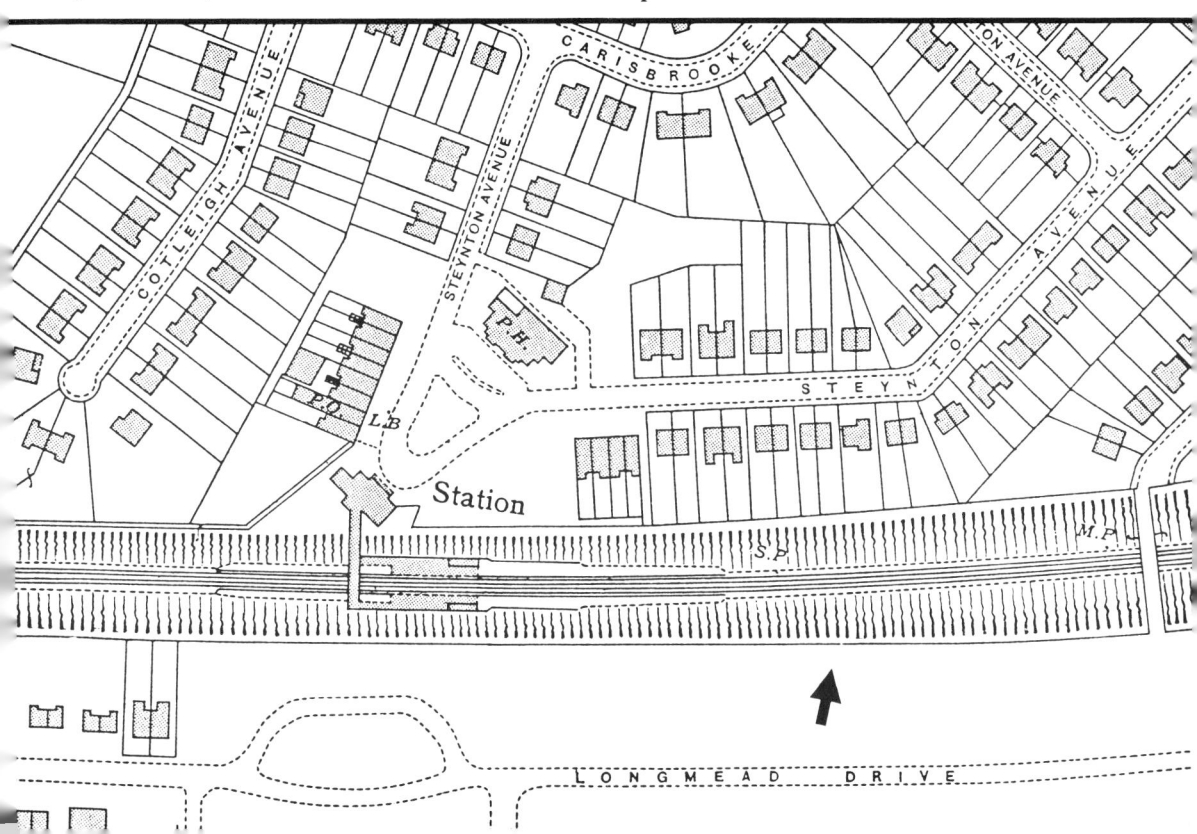

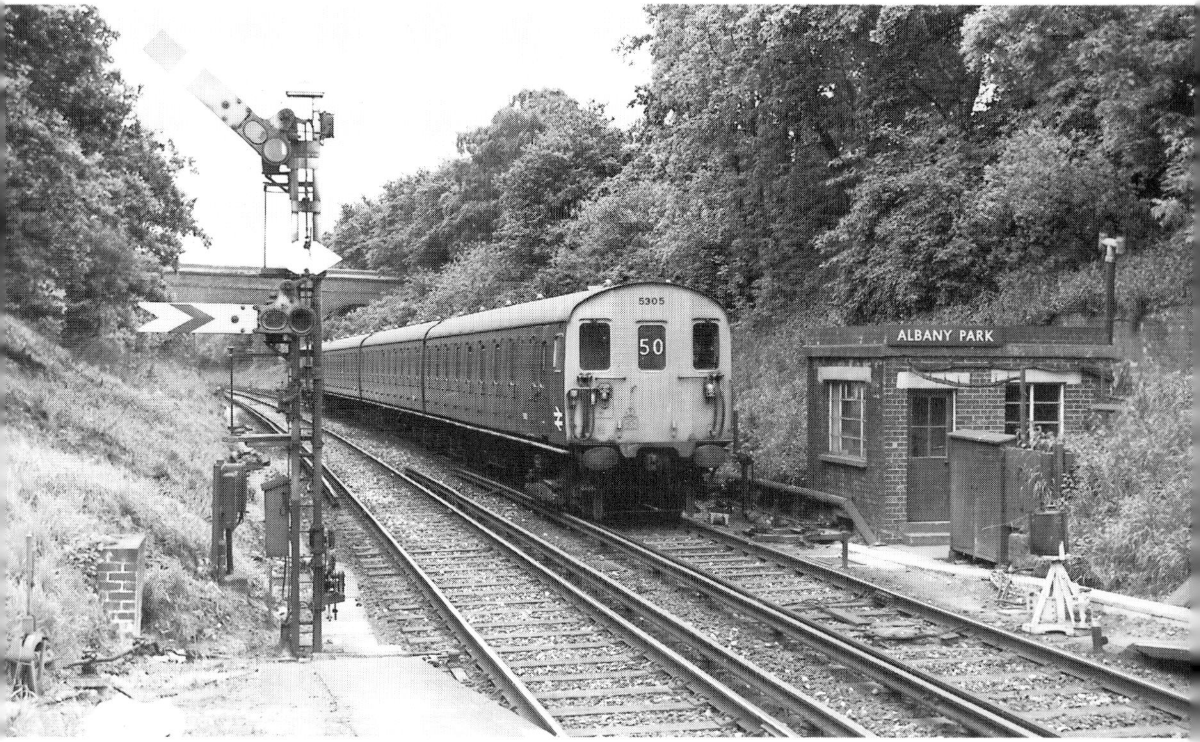
5305
50
ALBANY PARK

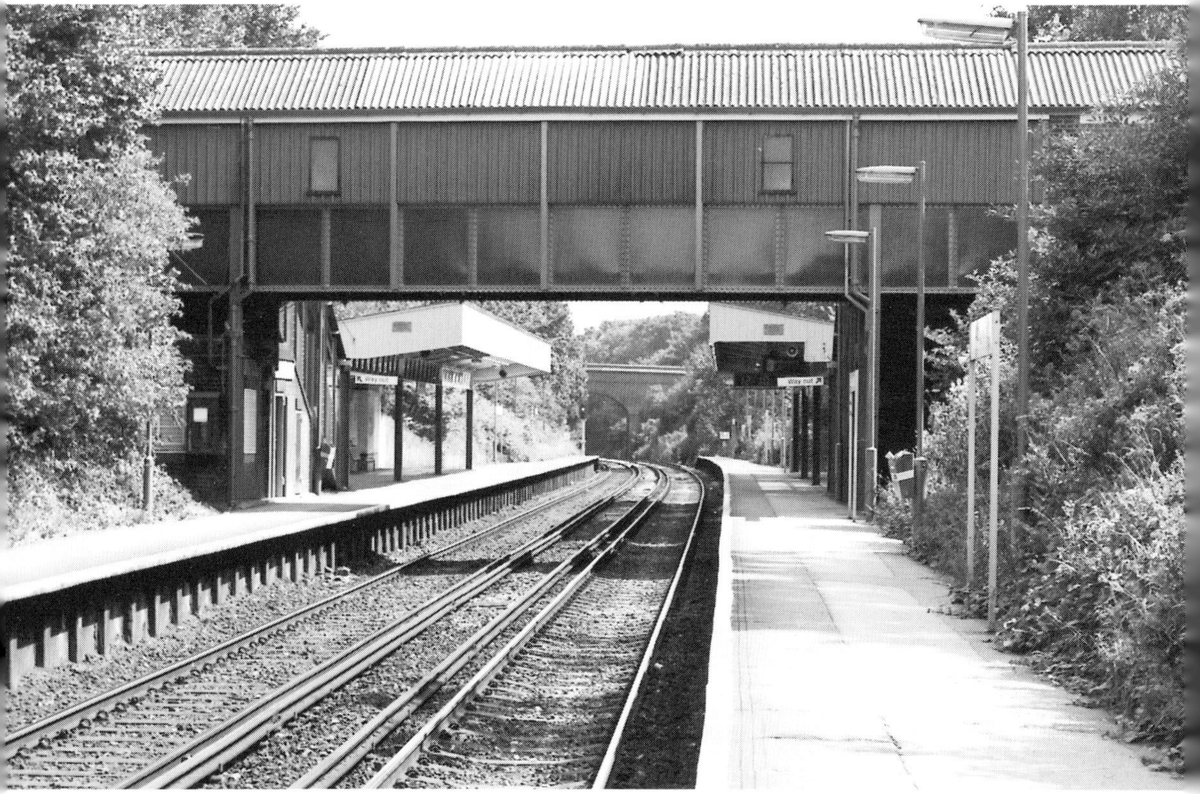

93. The 13.02 Dartford to Charing Cross approaches the station on 5th June 1969 and passes the tiny signal box, which had opened with the station and closed on 1st November 1970. The lever on the extreme left was for placing fog detonators - strange that it was not placed in the box, but fog signalling was not part of a signalman's duty. (J.Scrace)

94. An eastward view in 1990 includes mostly SR features, although the nameboards and lampposts are of more recent date. The footbridge roof sheeting appears to have been applied from each end so that the ridge capping does not fit. (J.Scrace)

95. No freight facilities were provided but much has passed through, such as the 9.40 Purley to Cliffe service on 9th August 1990, the locomotives being nos. 33063 and 33207. In view of the environment, it is little wonder that there are leaves on the line in autumn. (J.Scrace)

BEXLEY

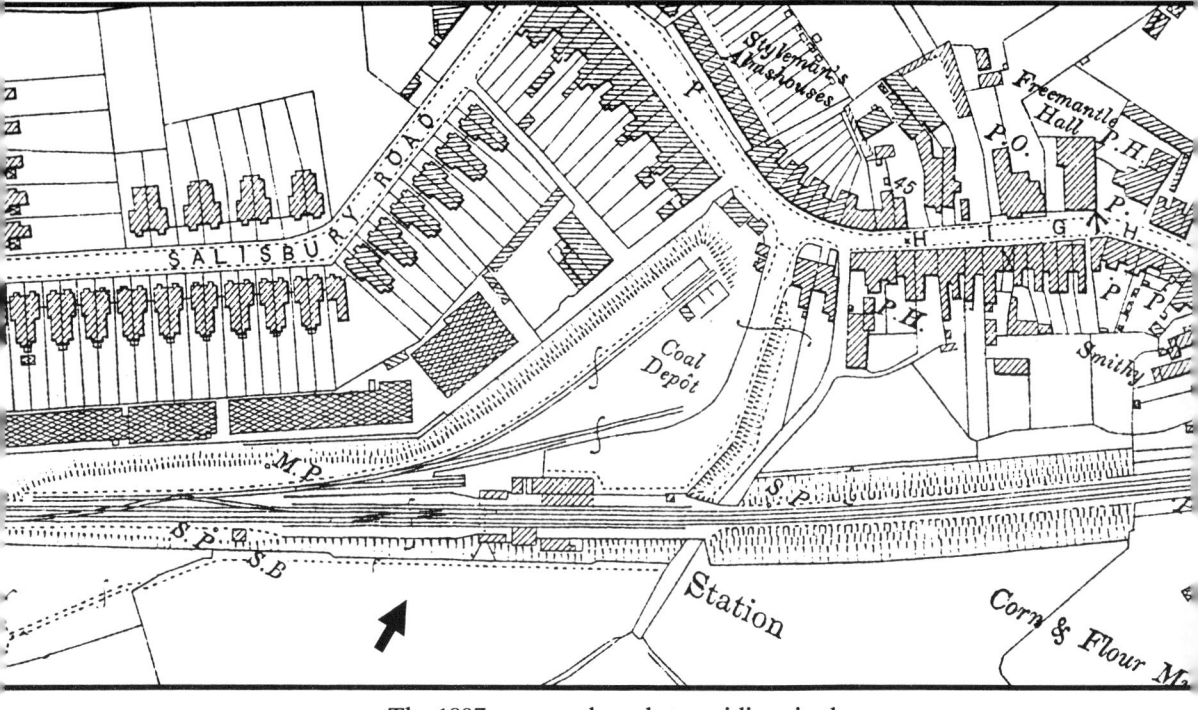

The 1897 map marks only two sidings in the coal yard but extensive glasshouses alongside it. As a result the glass probably needed frequent cleaning.

96. This classical view of the down side also includes interesting details of the goods yard signalling and the loading gauge. The fashions and advertisements are also worth studying. (Lens of Sutton)

97. All, except one safety-conscious trackman, look at the camera as F class 4-4-0 no. 24 approaches the up platform, the canopy of which is devoid of end valances, probably for reasons of signal sighting. (Lens of Sutton)

98. In their early years, both routes conveyed much produce from horticulturalists but this gradually reduced as the land was given over to housing and recreational use. This is a rare view of strawberry loading in Bexley Yard. The 4-4-0 is an F class. (Lens of Sutton)

99. The coaches are passing over the High Street as H class 0-4-4T no. A324 approaches the up platform on 13th March 1926. The double acting arms of the down starting signals helped to overcome sighting problems created by footbridges and canopies - the latter in this case (H.C.Casserley)

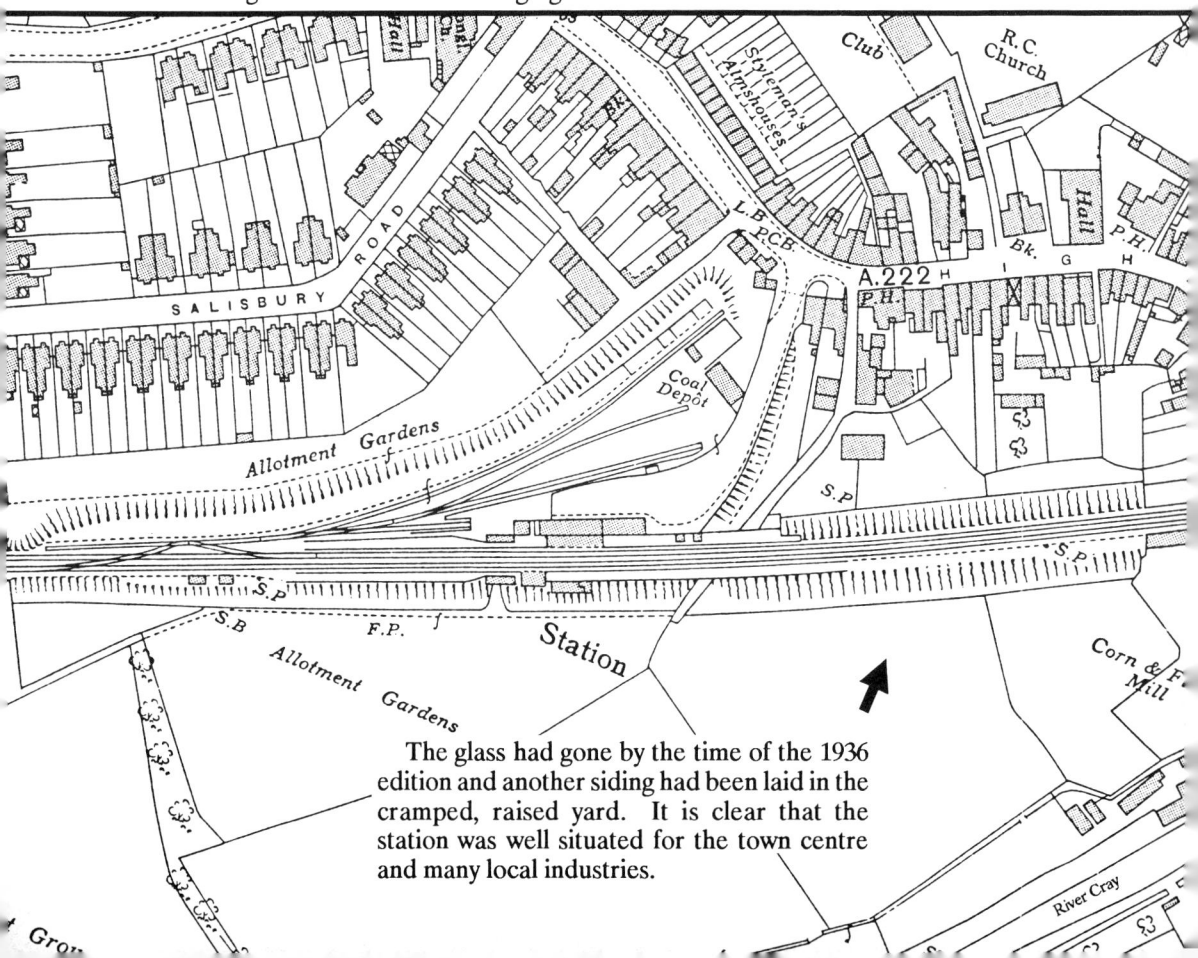

The glass had gone by the time of the 1936 edition and another siding had been laid in the cramped, raised yard. It is clear that the station was well situated for the town centre and many local industries.

100. When photographed in 1967, Bexley had lost 7% of its business passenger traffic to London over the previous 17 years, the overcrowding problem thus easing slightly. The general decline in commuting continued until 1984 but the losses since 1970 were completely restored by 1988. (J.N.Faulkner)

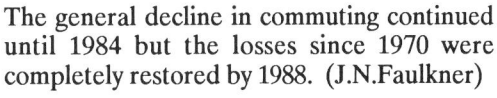

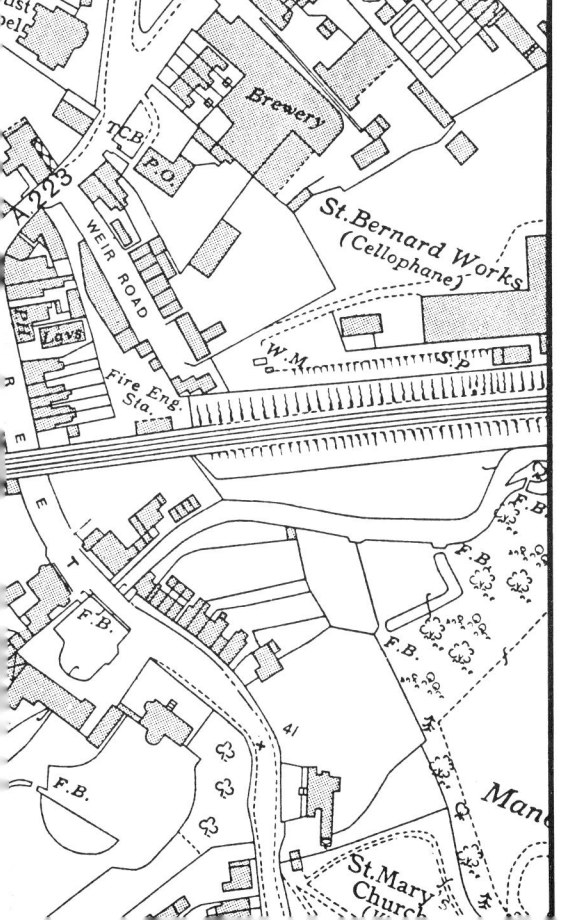

101. The traditional SER signal box, which closed on 1st November 1970, was situated opposite the goods yard from which traffic was withdrawn on 7th May 1963. The temporary speed restrictions may have been due to embankment instability - a common problem on both routes. (J.Scrace)

102. The subway approaches and other structures are seen in 1969, since when little has changed at this important station. The staff crossing has gone in the interest of safety. (J.Scrace)

103. The SER standardised their buildings (including signal boxes) on timber frames, weather boards and sash windows. Bexley is one of a few notable survivors and is seen complete with granite setts on which horse-drawn cabs once waited for custom. (C.Hall)

EAST OF BEXLEY

Near milepost 15, marked M.P. on this 1909 map, Crayford Brick Siding ran south to sandpits, passing over a three-arch brick bridge on its half-mile journey. Also marked is a locomotive shed which once housed a Hunslet 0-4-0ST. The line was lifted in 1931.

104. With collector shoes lowered, no. 73119 *Kentish Mercury* passes the sand and ballast pits on 22nd October 1986, with the Carlisle to Dover Speedlink service. The chemical tankers and other wagons will have destinations in mainland Europe, via the train ferry. (C.Wilson)

105. Adding to the diversity of freight on the route is gypsum from Mountfield, near Robertsbridge, to Northfleet in North Kent. This material is an ingredient in cement. No. 47367 is seen on 11th July 1990. (J.Scrace)

CRAYFORD

The 1938 map at 6" to 1 mile has Crayford station to the left of the fold. On the lower border of the left page is the pit at which the Crayford Brick Siding terminated. Part of its embankment is shown. To the right, a TRAMWAY is marked, this being a narrow gauge line which ended at a loading ramp at the southern extremity of a curved siding from Crayford station. Another standard gauge siding at the west end of the station was used for coal to the Wanshunt Pumping Station. East of Crayford station, a trailing siding enters an industrial complex which included Vickers Works. Their line extended north-east for ½ mile to the Flour Mills and Ply Works, serving another factory on the way. A double track spur between the lines marked DARTFORD LOOP and NORTH KENT LINE was opened on 11th October 1942 to facilitate movement of trains to and from Woolwich Arsenal. It ran across Crayford Marshes and is in use today, mainly for empty trains. On the right is Slade Green Depot, which had not been an engine shed since 1926. At the top of the right page is Slade Green station and at the top left of it is the Bexleyheath Line. On the lower part of the triangle, Braby's siding was added, this carrying a considerable traffic (tube, pipe and plate steel). Rutter's sidings are shown on the right, north of Crayford Creek. Later they had additional sidings west of the main line, these also being used by Dusseks Oils, who had bright blue tankers.

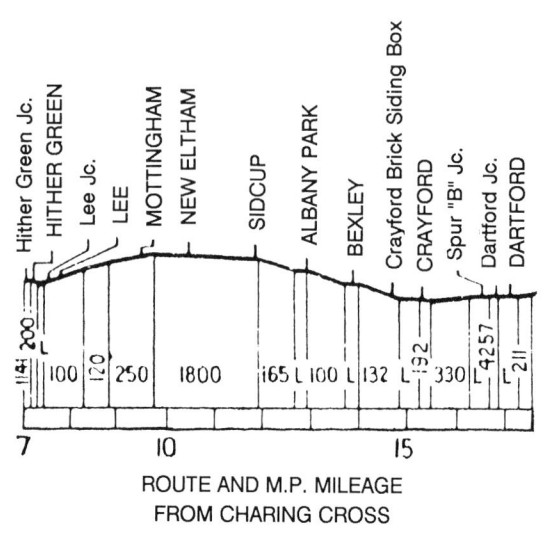

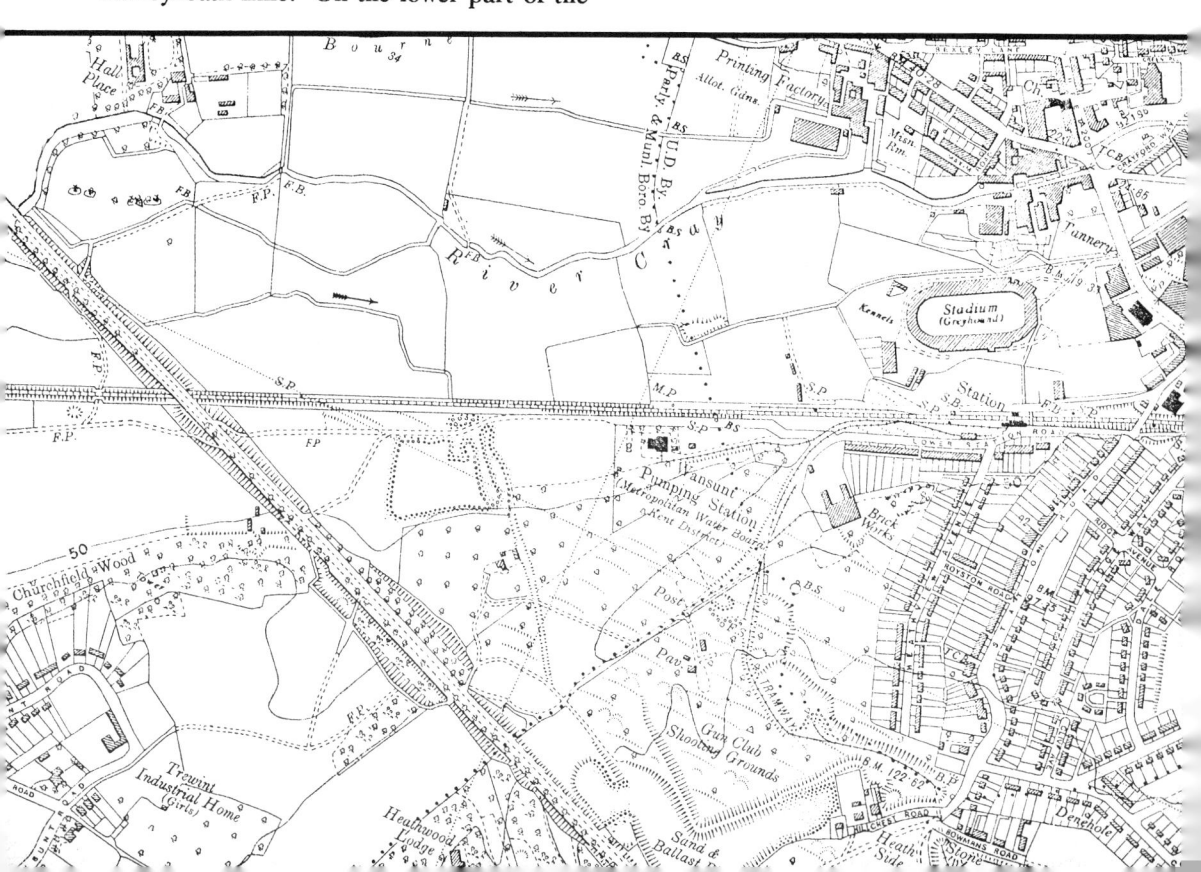

ROUTE AND M.P. MILEAGE
FROM CHARING CROSS

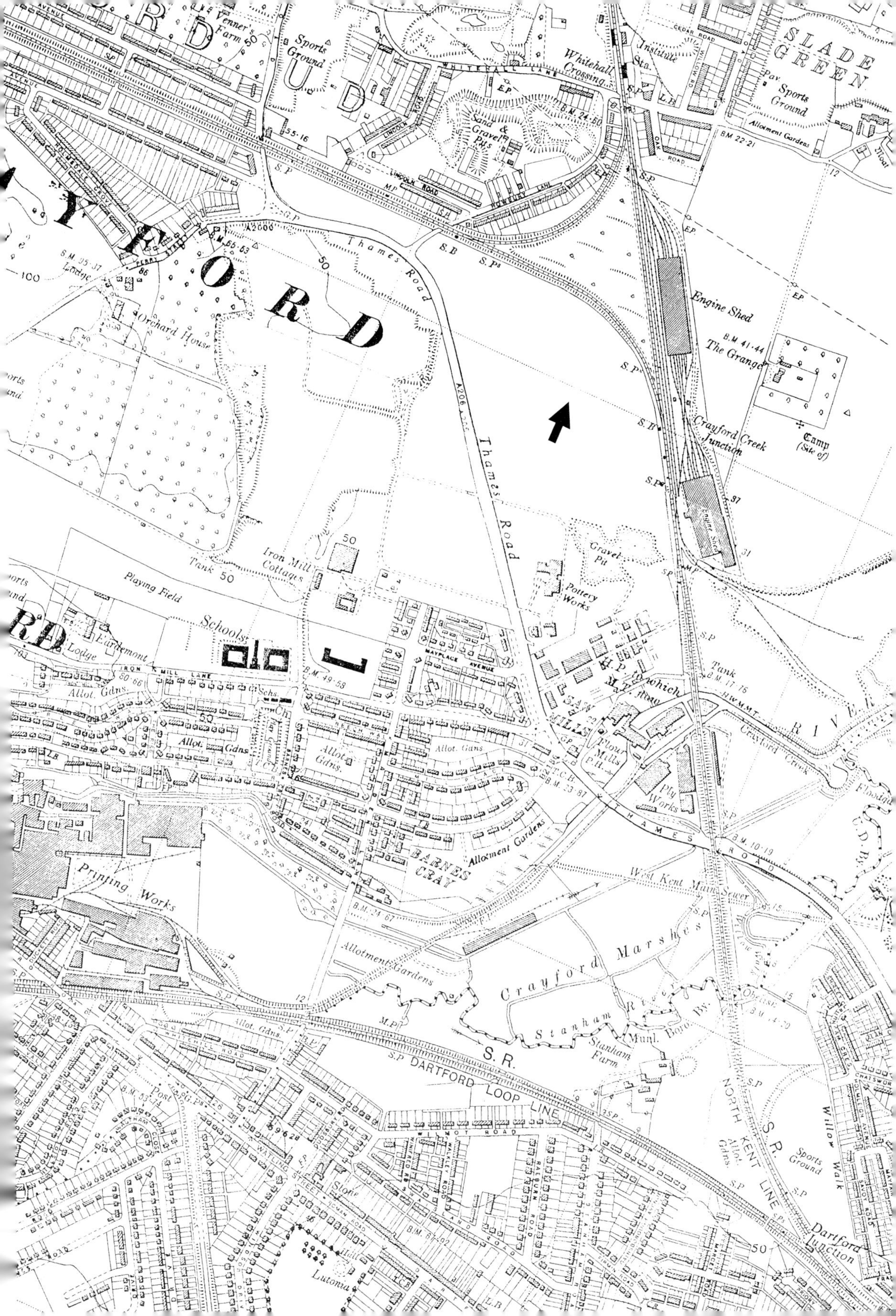

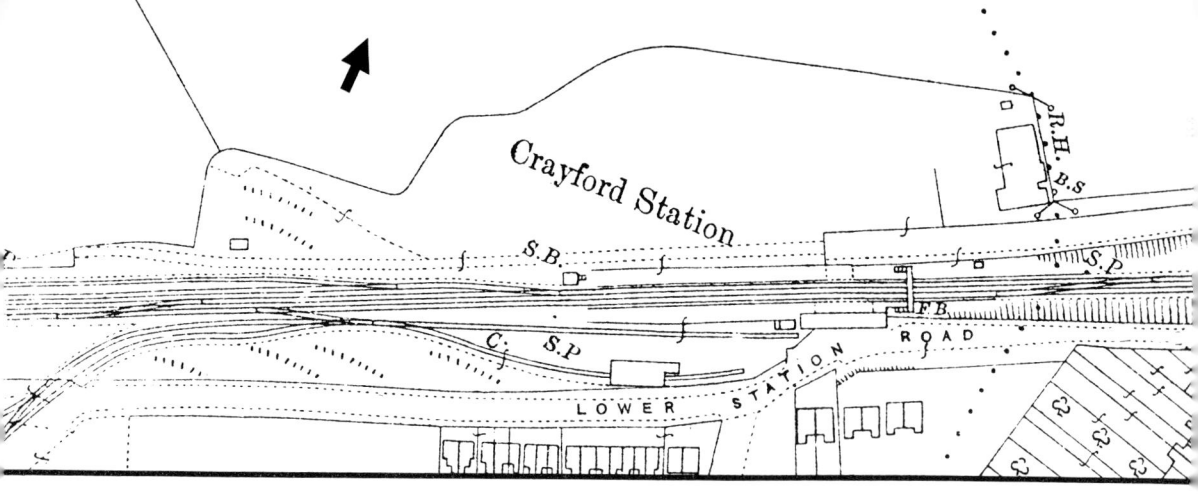

The 1933 survey has the private sidings to the waterworks and to the brickworks lower left. There is a small goods shed, a 4-ton crane and a siding on the down side, this being the only one initially.

106. Looking east in April 1953, we see coal wagons in the small yard and gaslamps still in use. As at many other stations on the routes, the undulating land restricted expansion of the goods yard. (D.Cullum)

CRAYFORD.

Crayford Sand and gravel and Metropolitan Water Board Wansunt pumping station sidings.—Two gates are provided across the lines at the entrance to the Crayford sand and gravel pits siding, and another at the entrance to the Wansunt pumping station siding, which leads out of the former.

Although the shunting may only be required in connection with the Crayford sand and gravel pits siding, the gate across the entrance to the Wansunt pumping station siding must also be opened during the shunting of the former.

The responsibility for the protection of persons using the roadway, which is crossed by the sidings, rests with the siding owners, but shunting movements over the roadway in question must be carried out with caution.

CRAYFORD BRICK COMPANY'S SIDING BETWEEN CRAYFORD & BEXLEY.—Crayford to send a Signalman for each Train calling at this Siding to open the Cabin as a Block Signalling Station.

107. A westward view from the road bridge in 1954 includes the goods shed and the signal box. In 1897, a loop was added nearby to give connection with a contractor's railway associated with the building of an asylum, one mile south of the line. (B.Nunns/A.Mott coll.)

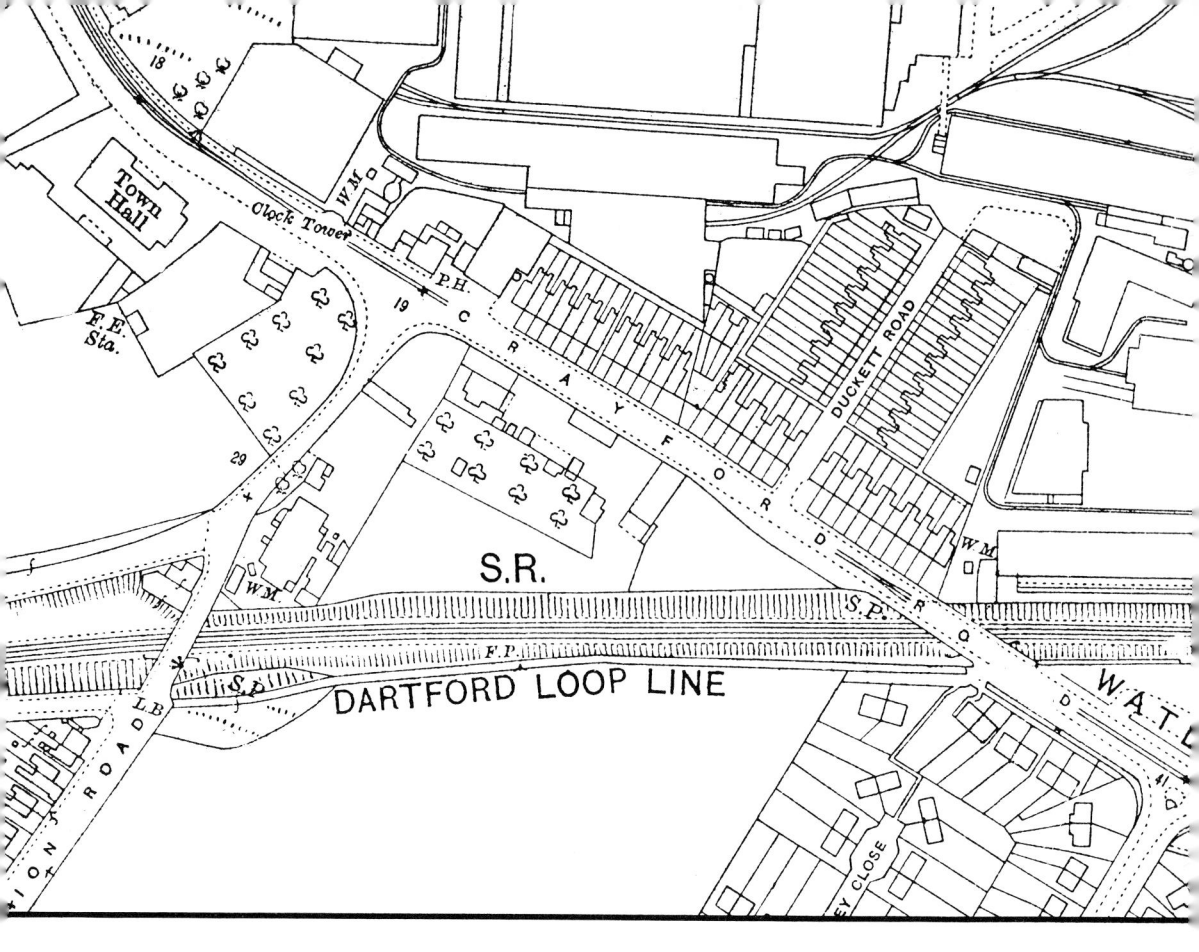

108. With the 15¼ milepost visible, the typical SER box was in use until 1st November 1970, its western neighbour, Crayford Brick Siding, having closed on 31st March 1931. This photograph dates from May 1967. (J.Scrace)

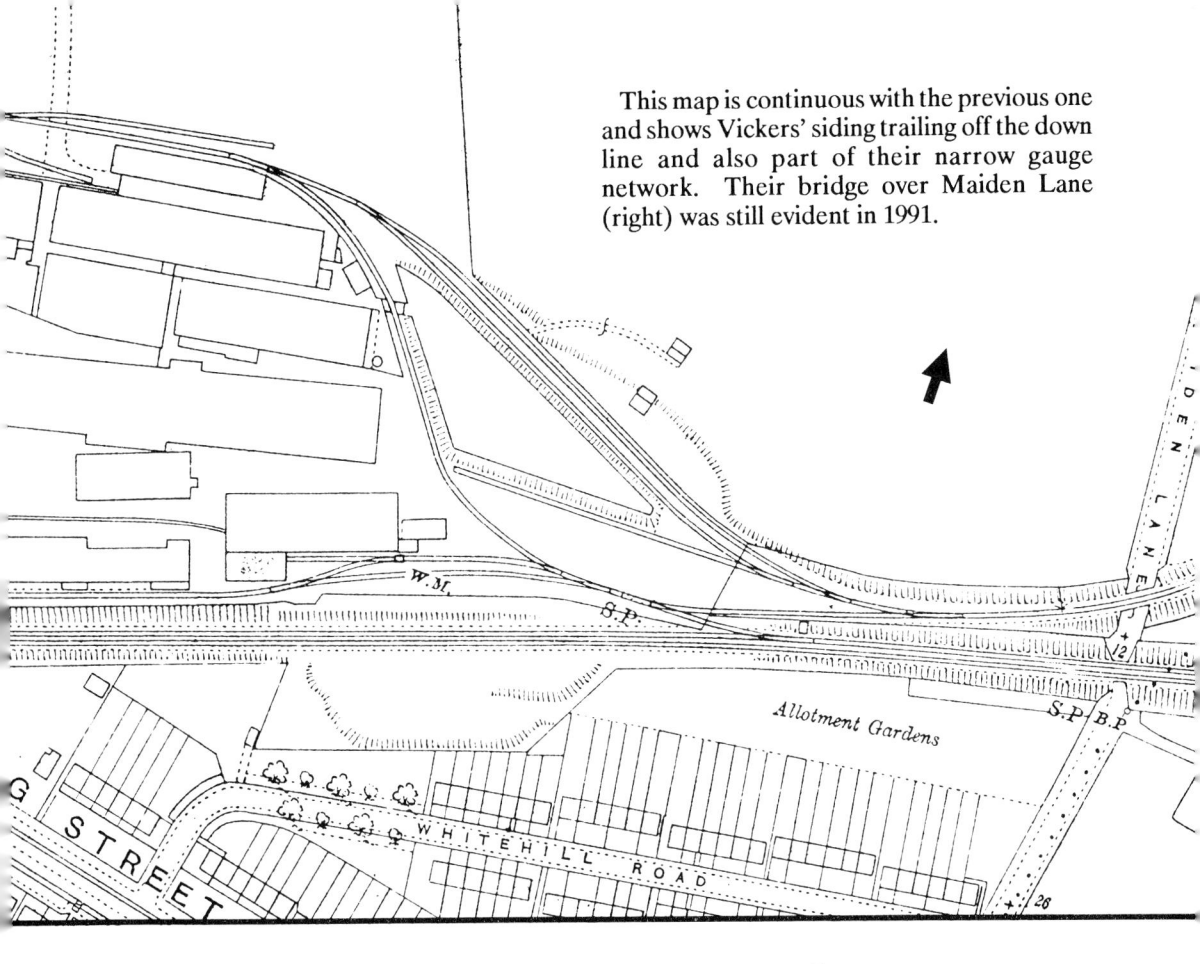

This map is continuous with the previous one and shows Vickers' siding trailing off the down line and also part of their narrow gauge network. Their bridge over Maiden Lane (right) was still evident in 1991.

109. Roadstone is another commodity regularly carried over the route. No. 56055 runs west with empties from Allington, near Maidstone, to Stoke Gifford, near Bristol on 10th January 1987. (C.Wilson)

110. The shabby old timber building was replaced by a dreary CLASP structure in 1969 - at least it was cleaner. Many of these temporary looking stations are being replaced by some imaginative architecture - a good example being at Oxford. (J.Scrace)

111. Flowerless flower tubs break the boredom slightly in the spring of 1990. At the far end of the platforms a crossover is available for terminating trains. (J.Scrace)

EAST OF CRAYFORD

112. Crayford Marshes are in the background and the signalling is in transition. The typical WWII box was in use from 11th October 1942 until 1st November 1970 and was named "Crayford Spur B Junction". (J.Scrace)

113. Dartford Junction also closed on 1st November 1970, when Dartford Panel took control of the area. Three tracks ran from here to Dartford, the centre one being signalled for reversible running since 1970. (J.Scrace)

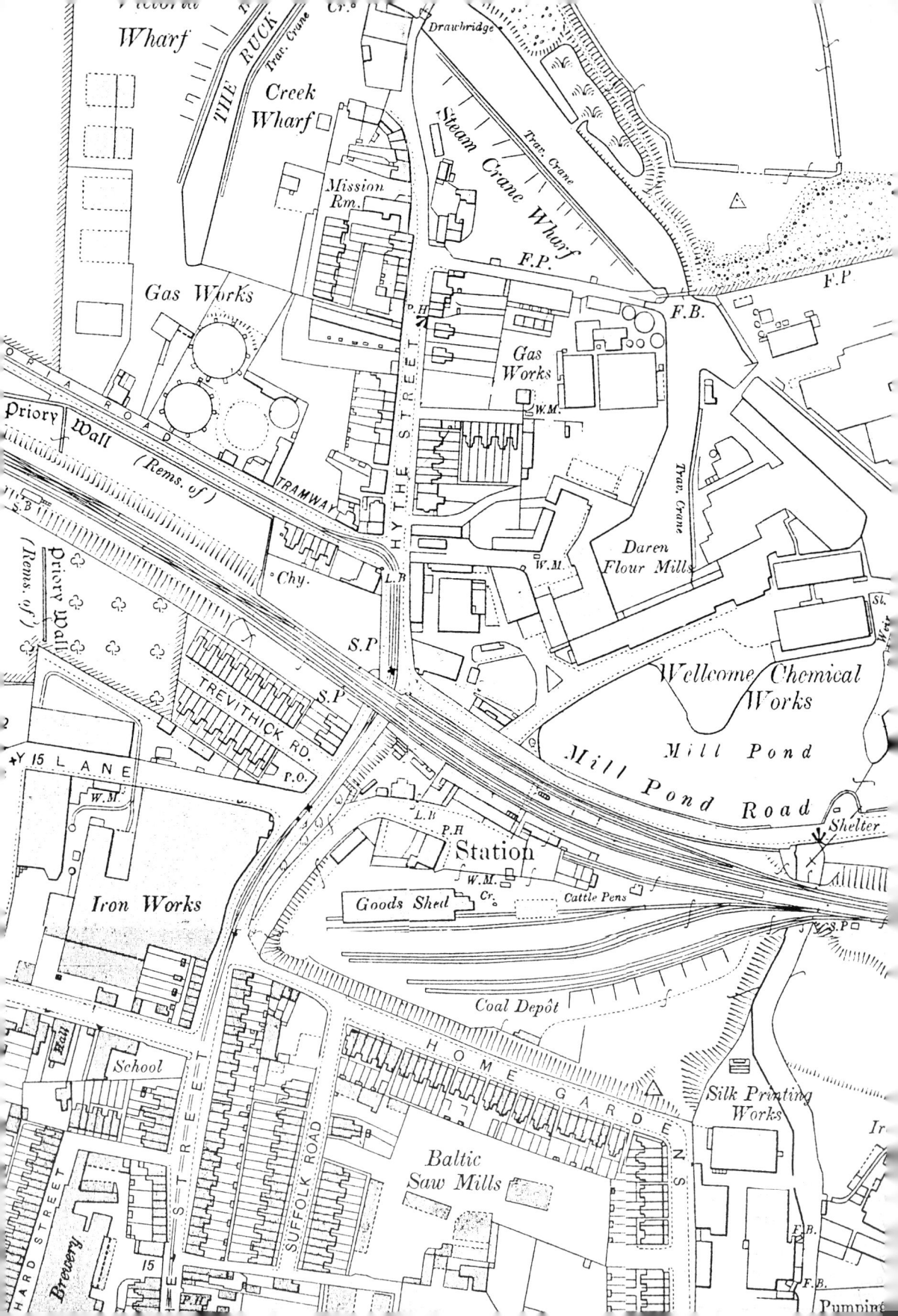

Wharf
Victoria Wharf
THE RUCK
Trav. Crane
Cr.
Drawbridge
Creek Wharf
Trav. Crane
Steam Crane Wharf
Trav. Crane
Mission Rm.
F.P.
F.P.
Gas Works
F.B.
Gas Works
W.M.
Priory Wall (Rems. of)
TRAMWAY
HYTHE STREET
Trav. Crane
W.M.
Daren Flour Mills
Chy.
L.B.
Weir
S.P.
Wellcome Chemical Works
Priory Wall (Rems. of)
TREVITHICK RD.
S.P.
Mill Pond
P.O.
Mill Pond Road
15 LANE
W.M.
L.B.
P.H.
Shelter
Station
W.M.
Goods Shed
Cr.
Cattle Pens
Iron Works
S.P.
Coal Depôt
Hall
School
HOME GARDENS
Silk Printing Works
STREET
SUFFOLK ROAD
Baltic Saw Mills
HARD STREET
Brewery
15
P.H.
F.B.
F.B.
Pumping
Ir

DARTFORD

The 1909 edition has three tracks (left) from Dartford Junction, the third one having come into use in about 1897. The centre track was used for down trains from Crayford, all up trains using the southern track.

114. Up trains could start from any of the three platforms. H class no. 520 is leaving from platform 2 on 24th April 1926, by which time the conductor rails were in place ready for the imminent electrification. (H.C.Casserely)

115. After electrification steam working was infrequent. Here we witness an example as class B1 no. 1448 has just arrived with a van train on 26th April 1947 and is seen at the entrance to the goods yard. (R.C.Riley)

116. An eastward view in 1953 from platform 1 shows the narrow and inconvenient island platform along with some of the SER timber clad buildings, which probably dated from the opening of the station on 30th July 1849. (D.Cullum)

117. Still looking east in 1953 but from the east end of platform 1, we see (on the right) the sidings of the goods yard which closed on 1st May 1972. In the distance is No. 2 Box, which remained in use until colour light signals were introduced in 1970. (D.Cullum)

118. The up semaphore signals were near the end of their life when photographed on 1st September 1970. On 1st November, Dartford Panel took over the work of 31 signal boxes and controlled 257 signals. Until 13th June 1954, No. 1 Box had been in use and was situated behind the camera and on the left of the map. (J.Scrace)

119. The viaduct had been widened in about 1867, 1897 and yet again in 1972. The last increase allowed the construction of two full width island platforms, which came into use on 5th August 1973. All four lines were signalled for reversible running and were photographed in June 1989. (J.Scrace)

For further illustrations of this station please see our companion album *Charing Cross to Dartford*, which covers the route via Greenwich and Woolwich.

120. Not only does Dartford see a variety of through freight services but this train of empty PCA cement tankers is reversing here, having arrived from Hoo Junction. No. 73110 has just run round and is about to depart for Swanscombe Cement Works. Amidst this activity eight passenger trains normally leave for London every hour, a remarkably good service. (C.Wilson)

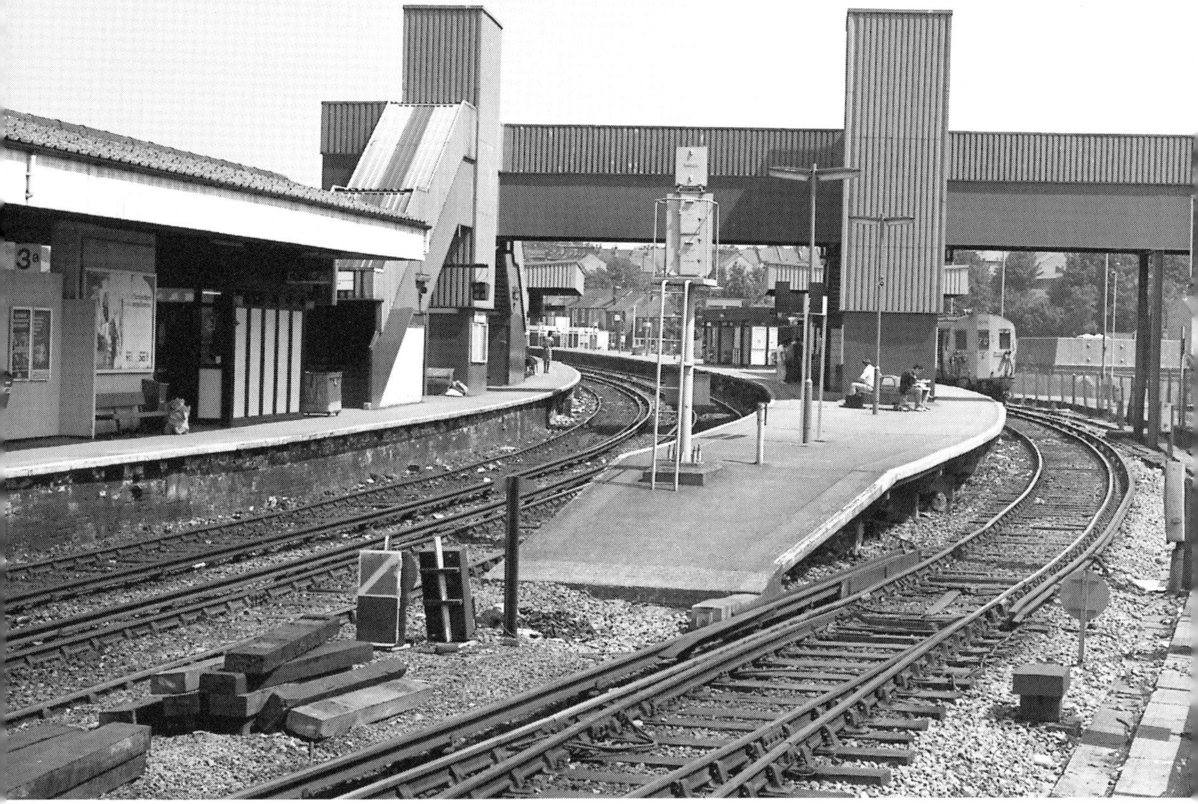
3a

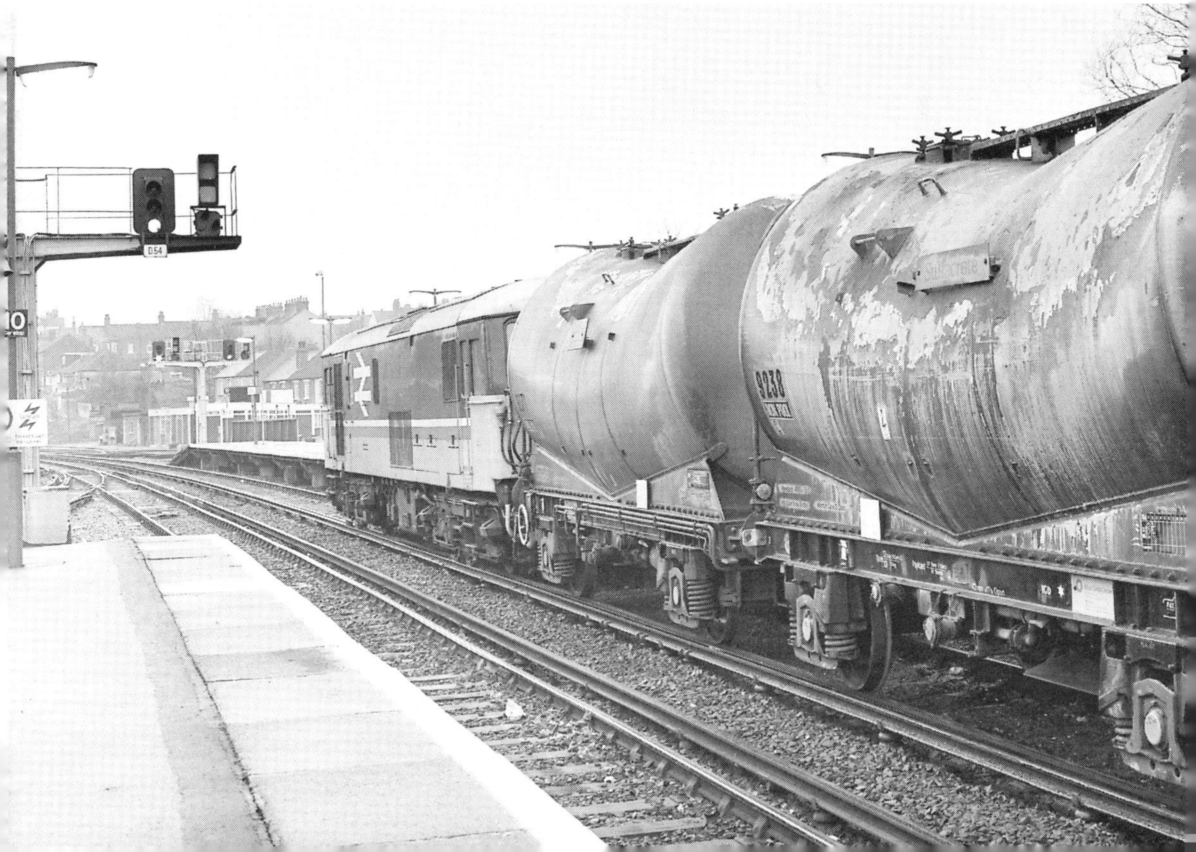
D54
9238

MP Middleton Press

Easebourne Lane, Midhurst. West Sussex. GU29 9AZ
(0730) 813169
Write or telephone for our latest booklist

BRANCH LINES

BRANCH LINES TO MIDHURST
BRANCH LINES AROUND MIDHURST
BRANCH LINES TO HORSHAM
BRANCH LINE TO SELSEY
BRANCH LINES TO EAST GRINSTEAD
BRANCH LINES TO ALTON
BRANCH LINE TO TENTERDEN
BRANCH LINES TO NEWPORT
BRANCH LINES TO TUNBRIDGE WELLS
BRANCH LINE TO SWANAGE
BRANCH LINE TO LYME REGIS
BRANCH LINE TO FAIRFORD
BRANCH LINE TO ALLHALLOWS
BRANCH LINES AROUND ASCOT
BRANCH LINES AROUND WEYMOUTH
BRANCH LINE TO HAWKHURST
BRANCH LINES AROUND EFFINGHAM JN
BRANCH LINE TO MINEHEAD
BRANCH LINE TO SHREWSBURY
BRANCH LINES AROUND HUNTINGDON

SOUTH COAST RAILWAYS

CHICHESTER TO PORTSMOUTH
BRIGHTON TO EASTBOURNE
RYDE TO VENTNOR
EASTBOURNE TO HASTINGS
PORTSMOUTH TO SOUTHAMPTON
HASTINGS TO ASHFORD
SOUTHAMPTON TO BOURNEMOUTH
ASHFORD TO DOVER
BOURNEMOUTH TO WEYMOUTH
DOVER TO RAMSGATE

SOUTHERN MAIN LINES

HAYWARDS HEATH TO SEAFORD
EPSOM TO HORSHAM
CRAWLEY TO LITTLEHAMPTON
THREE BRIDGES TO BRIGHTON
WATERLOO TO WOKING
VICTORIA TO EAST CROYDON
EAST CROYDON TO THREE BRIDGES
WOKING TO SOUTHAMPTON
WATERLOO TO WINDSOR
LONDON BRIDGE TO EAST CROYDON
BASINGSTOKE TO SALISBURY
SITTINGBOURNE TO RAMSGATE
YEOVIL TO EXETER

COUNTRY RAILWAY ROUTES

BOURNEMOUTH TO EVERCREECH JN
READING TO GUILDFORD
WOKING TO ALTON
BATH TO EVERCREECH JUNCTION
GUILDFORD TO REDHILL
EAST KENT LIGHT RAILWAY
FAREHAM TO SALISBURY
BURNHAM TO EVERCREECH JUNCTION
REDHILL TO ASHFORD
YEOVIL TO DORCHESTER
ANDOVER TO SOUTHAMPTON

LONDON SUBURBAN RAILWAYS

CHARING CROSS TO DARTFORD
HOLBORN VIADUCT TO LEWISHAM
KINGSTON & HOUNSLOW LOOPS
CRYSTAL PALACE AND CATFORD LOOP

STEAMING THROUGH

STEAMING THROUGH EAST HANTS
STEAMING THROUGH SURREY
STEAMING THROUGH WEST SUSSEX
STEAMING THROUGH THE ISLE OF WIGHT
STEAMING THROUGH WEST HANTS

OTHER RAILWAY BOOKS

GARRAWAY FATHER & SON
LONDON CHATHAM & DOVER RAILWAY
INDUSTRIAL RAILWAYS OF THE S. EAST
WEST SUSSEX RAILWAYS IN THE 1980s
SOUTH EASTERN RAILWAY

OTHER BOOKS

WALKS IN THE WESTERN HIGH WEALD
TILLINGBOURNE BUS STORY

MILITARY DEFENCE OF WEST SUSSEX
BATTLE OVER SUSSEX 1940

SURREY WATERWAYS
KENT AND EAST SUSSEX WATERWAYS
HAMPSHIRE WATERWAYS